easy to make!

Soups

Good Housekeeping

easy to make!

Soups

COLLINS & BROWN

First published in Great Britain in 2009
by Collins & Brown
10 Southcombe Street
London W14 0RA

An imprint of Anova Books Company Ltd

The Good Housekeeping website is
www.allboutyou.com/goodhousekeeping

1 2 3 4 5 6 7 8 9

ISBN 978-1-84340-550-4

A catalogue record for this book is available from the British
Library.

Reproduction by Dot Gradations UK, Ltd
Printed and bound by Times Offset, Malaysia

This book can be ordered direct from the publisher. Contact the
marketing department, but try your bookshop first.

www.anovabooks.com

NOTES

- Both metric and imperial measures are given for the
  recipes. Follow either set of measures, not a mixture
  of both, as they are not interchangeable.
- All spoon measures are level.
  1 tsp = 5ml spoon; 1 tbsp = 15ml spoon.
- Ovens and grills must be preheated to the specified
  temperature.
- Use sea salt and freshly ground black pepper unless
  otherwise suggested.
- Fresh herbs should be used unless dried herbs are
  specified in a recipe.
- Medium eggs should be used except where
  otherwise specified. Free-range eggs are
  recommended.
- Note that certain recipes, including mayonnaise,
  lemon curd and some cold desserts, contain raw or
  lightly cooked eggs. The young, elderly, pregnant
  women and anyone with an immune-deficiency
  disease should avoid these, because of the slight risk
  of salmonella.
- Calorie, fat and carbohydrate counts per serving are
  provided for the recipes.

Picture credits
Photographers: Neil Barclay (page 66); Nicki Dowey (32, 36, 38,
39, 40, 42, 44, 45, 46, 47, 49, 50, 51, 58, 59, 60, 61, 64, 65, 67,
68, 69, 72, 73, 74, 76, 77, 79, 80, 81, 82, 83, 85, 87, 87, 88, 92,
93, 94, 97, 99, 100, 101, 102, 104, 105, 107, 110, 112, 115, 117,
119, 120, 123, 126); Craig Robertson (Basics photography plus
pages 33, 34, 35, 41, 54, 56, 57, 63, 73, 76, 111, 118. 124);
Lucinda Symons (pages 28, 96, 122).

Contents

Foreword

There are few recipes more satisfying than soup. It can be rich and warming on a cold winter's day or chilled and refreshing to cool you down in the heat of summer. When you're pushed for time, it's the ultimate quick-fix supper. It can be prepared and on the table in half an hour – a chunk of bread and good wedge of cheese will complete the meal. Having friends round? Soup is a perfect starter. Easy to make and dress up – serve with croutons then simply finish with a sprinkling of finely chopped herbs and a swirl of cream.

It's a great moneysaver, too. This is the time to make the most of those odds and ends and leftover vegetables at the end of the week. Throw them into the pan with hot stock – chicken or vegetable work best – with lentils or canned beans and simmer until tender. Leave it chunky for a hearty feast or purée until smooth in a blender if you prefer. Whichever way, this is the ultimate storecupboard meal.

For new inspiration I'm going to be flicking through this book. My favourites so far are the almost instant easy pea soup – start with a bag of frozen peas and add hot stock – and the creamed celeriac and fresh parmesan soup. This is a luxurious blend of root vegetables, topped with parmesan crisps. Easy to do but impressive enough to wow guests at the next dinner party. Whichever dish you choose, we're sure you'll enjoy it. All the recipes are triple-tested in the Good Housekeeping Institute to make sure they work every time for you.

Karen

Karen Barnes
Head of the Good Housekeeping Institute
Good Housekeeping

0

The Basics

Making soups

Soups are nutritious, full of flavour and easy to make. Incredibly versatile, they can be smooth or chunky, light for a first course or substantial for a main course, made with vegetables, pulses, meat, chicken or fish.

Puréeing soups

1 **Using a jug blender** Allow the soup to cool slightly, then fill the jug about half-full, making sure that there is more liquid than solids. Cover the lid with a teatowel and hold it on tightly. Blend until smooth, then add more solids and blend again until all the soup is smooth. (If you have a lot of soup, transfer each batch to a clean pan.)

2 **Using a stick blender** Allow the soup to cool slightly. Stick the blender deep into the soup, switch it on and move it about so that all the soup is puréed.
Note: don't do this in a non-stick pan.

3 **Using a mouli** A mouli-légumes makes a fine purée, although it takes longer than using a blender. Fit the fine plate to the mouli-légumes and set it over a bowl – put a teatowel underneath to keep it from moving on the table. Fill the bowl of the mouli about halfway up the sides, putting in more solids than liquid. Work in batches if you have a large quantity of soup.

4 **Using a sieve** If you don't have a blender or mouli-légumes, you can purée soup by pushing it through a sieve, although this will take a much longer time.

Partially puréed soups

1 For an interesting texture, purée one-third to half of the ingredients, then stir back into the soup.

2 Alternatively, prepare the vegetables or other ingredients, but set aside a few choice pieces. While the soup is cooking, steam or boil these pieces until just tender; refresh green vegetables in cold water. Just before serving, cut into smaller pieces and add to the soup.

Chunky soups

1 Cut the ingredients into bite-size pieces. Heat oil or butter in the soup pan and cook the onions – and garlic if you like – until soft and lightly coloured.

2 Add the remaining ingredients, putting in those that need the longest cooking first. Pour in some stock and bring to the boil.

3 Simmer gently until all the ingredients are tender. If too much liquid boils away, just add more.

Simple Vegetable Soup

You can use almost any mixture of vegetables.
To serve four, you will need:
1 or 2 finely chopped onions, 2 tbsp oil or 1 tbsp oil and 25g (1oz) butter, 1 or 2 crushed garlic cloves (optional), 450g (1lb) chopped mixed vegetables, such as leeks, potatoes, celery, fennel, canned tomatoes and parsnips (chopped finely or cut into larger dice for a chunky soup), 1.1 litres (2 pints) stock.

1 Fry the onions in the oil or oil and butter until soft and add the garlic if you like.

2 Add the chopped mixed vegetables and the stock. Bring to the boil and simmer for 20–30 minutes until the vegetables are tender.

3 Leave chunky, partially purée or blend until smooth.

Making stock

Good stock can make the difference between a good soup and a great one. It also gives depth of flavour to many dishes. There are four main types of stock: vegetable, meat, chicken and fish.

Cook's Tips

- To get a clearer liquid when making fish, meat or poultry stock, strain the cooked stock through four layers of muslin in a sieve.
- Stock will keep for three days in the refrigerator. If you want to keep it for a further three days, transfer it to a pan and reboil gently for five minutes. Cool, put in a clean bowl and chill for a further three days.
- When making meat or chicken stock, make sure there is a good ratio of meat to bones. The more meat you use, the more flavour the stock will have.

Stocks

Vegetable Stock

For 1.2 litres (2 pints), you will need:
225g (8oz) each onions, celery, leeks and carrots, chopped, 1 bouquet garni (2 bay leaves, a few thyme sprigs, 1 small bunch of parsley), 10 black peppercorns, ½ tsp salt.

1 Put all the ingredients into a large pan and add 1.7 litres (3 pints) cold water. Bring slowly to the boil and skim the surface.

2 Partially cover the pan and simmer for 30 minutes. Adjust the seasoning if necessary. Strain the stock through a fine sieve into a bowl and leave to cool.

Meat Stock

For 900ml (1½ pints), you will need:
450g (1lb) each meat bones and stewing meat, 1 onion, 2 celery sticks and 1 large carrot, sliced, 1 bouquet garni (2 bay leaves, a few thyme sprigs, 1 small bunch of parsley), 1 tsp black peppercorns, ½ tsp salt.

1 Preheat the oven to 220°C (200°C fan oven) mark 7. Put the meat and bones into a roasting tin and roast for 30–40 minutes, turning now and again, until they are well browned.

2 Put the bones into a large pan with the remaining ingredients and add 2 litres (3½ pints) cold water. Bring slowly to the boil and skim the surface.

3 Partially cover the pan and simmer for 4–5 hours. Adjust the seasoning if necessary. Strain through a muslin-lined sieve into a bowl and cool quickly. Degrease (see opposite) before using.

Chicken Stock

For 1.2 litres (2 pints), you will need:
1.6kg (3½lb) chicken bones, 225g (8oz) each onions and celery, sliced, 150g (5oz) chopped leeks, 1 bouquet garni (2 bay leaves, a few thyme sprigs, 1 small bunch of parsley), 1 tsp black peppercorns, ½ tsp salt.

1 Put all the ingredients into a large pan and add 3 litres (5¼ pints) cold water. Bring slowly to the boil and skim the surface.

2 Partially cover the pan and simmer gently for 2 hours. Adjust the seasoning if necessary.

3 Strain the stock through a muslin-lined sieve into a bowl and cool quickly. Degrease (see right) before using.

Fish Stock

For 900ml (1½ pints), you will need:
900g (2lb) fish bones and trimmings, washed, 2 carrots, 1 onion and 2 celery sticks, sliced, 1 bouquet garni (2 bay leaves, a few thyme sprigs, 1 small bunch of parsley), 6 white peppercorns, ½ tsp salt.

1 Put all the ingredients into a large pan and add 900ml (1½ pints) cold water. Bring slowly to the boil and skim the surface.

2 Partially cover the pan and simmer gently for 30 minutes. Adjust the seasoning if necessary.

3 Strain through a muslin-lined sieve into a bowl and cool quickly. Fish stock tends not to have much fat in it and so does not usually need to be degreased. However, if it does seem to be fatty, you will need to remove this by degreasing it (see right).

Degreasing stock

Meat and poultry stock needs to be degreased. (Vegetable stock does not.) You can mop the fat from the surface using kitchen paper, but the following methods are easier and more effective. There are three main methods that you can use: ladling, pouring and chilling.

1 **Ladling** While the stock is warm, place a ladle on the surface. Press down and allow the fat floating on the surface to trickle over the edge until the ladle is full. Discard the fat, then repeat until all the fat has been removed.

2 **Pouring** For this you need a degreasing jug or a double-pouring gravy boat, which has the spout at the base of the vessel. When you fill the jug or gravy boat with a fatty liquid, the fat rises. When you pour, the stock comes out while the fat stays behind in the jug.

3 **Chilling** This technique works best with stock made from meat, as the fat solidifies when cold. Put the stock in the refrigerator until the fat becomes solid, then remove the pieces of fat using a slotted spoon.

Preparing vegetables

Vegetables form the basis of most soups – whether smooth or chunky – adding flavour and bulk. Here are some of the most popular vegetables and how to prepare them.

Onions

1 Cut off the tip and base of the onion. Peel away all the layers of papery skin and any discoloured layers underneath.

2 Put the onion root end down on the chopping board, then, using a sharp knife, cut the onion in half from tip to base.

3 Slicing Put one half on the board with the cut surface facing down and slice across the onion.

4 Chopping Slice the halved onions from the root end to the top at regular intervals. Next, make 2–3 horizontal slices through the onion, then slice vertically across the width.

Shallots

1 Cut off the tip and trim off the ends of the root. Peel off the skin and any discoloured layers underneath.

2 Holding the shallot with the root end down, use a small, sharp knife to make deep parallel slices almost down to the base while keeping the slices attached to it.

3 Slicing Turn the shallot on its side and cut off slices from the base.

4 Dicing Make deep parallel slices at right angles to the first slices. Turn the shallot on its side and cut off the slices from the base. You should now have fine dice, but chop any larger pieces individually.

Seeding tomatoes

1 Halve the tomato through the core. Use a spoon or a small sharp knife to remove the seeds and juice. Shake off the excess liquid.

2 Chop the tomato as required for your recipe and place in a colander for a minute or two, to drain off any excess liquid.

Cutting tomatoes

1 Use a small sharp knife to cut out the core in a single cone-shaped piece. Discard the core.

2 **Wedges** Halve the tomato and then cut into quarters or into three.

3 **Slices** Hold the tomato with the cored side on the chopping board for greater stability and use a serrated knife to cut into slices.

Seeding peppers

The seeds and white pith of peppers taste bitter so should be removed.

1 Cut off the top of the pepper, then cut away and discard the seeds and white pith.

2 Alternatively, cut the pepper in half vertically and snap out the white pithy core and seeds. Trim away the rest of the white membrane with a knife.

Chargrilling peppers

Charring imparts a smoky flavour and makes peppers easier to peel.

1 Hold the pepper, using tongs, over the gas flame on your hob (or under a preheated grill) until the skin blackens, turning until black all over.

2 Put into a bowl, cover and leave to cool (the steam will help to loosen the skin). Peel.

Peeling tomatoes

1 Fill a bowl or pan with boiling water. Using a slotted spoon, carefully add the tomato and leave for 15–30 seconds, then remove to a chopping board.

2 Use a small sharp knife to cut out the core in a single cone-shaped piece. Discard the core.

3 Peel off the skin; it should come away easily, depending on ripeness.

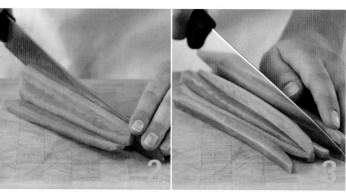

Carrots

1 First, peel and cut off the ends. Cut slices off each of the rounded sides to make four flat surfaces that are stable on the chopping board.

2 Hold steady with one hand and cut lengthways into even slices so they are lying in a flat stack.

3 To dice the shreds, turn the stack at right angles and cut through in the opposite direction.

Mushrooms

Button, white, chestnut and flat mushrooms are all prepared in a similar way.

1 Wipe with a damp cloth or pastry brush to remove any dirt.

2 With button mushrooms, cut off the stalk flush with the base of the cap. For other mushrooms, cut a thin disc off the end of the stalk and discard. Chop or slice the mushrooms.

Squash

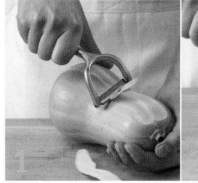

1 For steaming, baking or roasting, keep the chunks fairly large – at least 2.5cm (1in) thick. Peel with a swivel-handled peeler or a chef's knife.

2 Halve the squash, then use a knife to cut through some of the fibrous mass connecting the seeds with the wall of the central cavity. Scoop out the seeds and fibres with a spoon, then cut the flesh into pieces.

Leeks

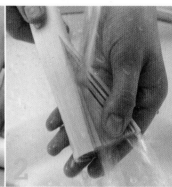

As some leeks harbour a lot of grit and earth between their leaves, they need careful cleaning.

1 Cut off the root and any tough parts of the leek. Make a cut into the leaf end of the leek, about 7.5cm (3in) deep.

2 Hold under the cold tap while separating the cut halves to expose any grit. Wash well, then shake dry. Use the green tops for stock.

Cabbage

The crinkly leaved Savoy cabbage may need more washing than other varieties, because its open leaves catch dirt more easily than the tightly packed white and red cabbage. The following method is suitable for all cabbages.

1 Pick off any of the outer leaves that are dry, tough or discoloured. Cut off the base and, using a small sharp knife, cut out as much as possible of the tough inner core in a single cone-shaped piece.

2 If you need whole cabbage leaves, peel them off one by one. As you work your way down, you will need to cut out more of the core.

3 If you are cooking the cabbage in wedges, cut it in half lengthways then cut the pieces into wedges of the required size.

Asparagus

Cut or snap off the woody stem of each asparagus spear about 5cm (2in) from the stalk end, or where the white and green sections meet. Or cut off the stalk end and peel with a vegetable peeler or small sharp knife.

Avocados

Prepare avocados just before using in a soup because their flesh discolours quickly once exposed to air.

1 Halve the avocado lengthways and twist the two halves apart. Tap the stone with a sharp knife, then twist to remove the stone.

2 Run a knife between the flesh and skin and pull away. Slice or chop the flesh as required.

Courgettes

Cutting diagonally is an ideal, all-purpose shape if using courgettes as a garnish for soup.

1 After washing under the cold tap, dry the courgette well and trim the base and the stem.

2 Trim off a piece at the base at a 45 degree angle, then repeat with the remaining courgette.

Spring onions

Cut off the roots and trim any coarse or withered green parts. Slice diagonally, or shred by cutting into 5cm (2in) lengths and then slicing down the lengths, or chop finely, according to the recipe.

Broccoli

1 Slice off the end of the stalk and cut 1cm (½in) below the florets.

2 Peel the thick, woody skin from the stalks and slice in half or quarters lengthways. Cut off equal-sized florets with a small knife. If the florets are very large you can halve them by cutting lengthways through the stalk and pulling the two halves apart.

Fennel

1 Trim off the top stems and the base of the bulbs. Remove the core with a small sharp knife if it seems tough.

2 The outer leaves may be discoloured and can be scrubbed gently in cold water, or you can peel away the discoloured parts with a knife or a vegetable peeler. Slice the fennel or cut it into quarters, according to your recipe.

Ginger

1 Grating Cut off a piece of the root and peel with a vegetable peeler. Cut off any brown spots.

2 Rest the grater on a board or small plate and grate the ginger. Discard any large fibres adhering to the pulp.

3 Slicing, shredding and chopping Cut slices off the ginger and cut off the skin carefully. Cut off any brown spots. Stack the slices and cut into shreds. To chop, stack the shreds and cut across into small pieces.

4 Pressing If you just need the ginger juice, peel and cut off any brown spots, then cut into small chunks and use a garlic press held over a small bowl to extract the juice.

Flavourings

Garlic, ginger and spring onions are the basic flavourings in many soups, especially the spicier ones. Many of these soups also include chillies, lemongrass or a prepared spice paste such as Thai curry paste.

Lemongrass

Lemongrass is a popular South-east Asian ingredient, giving an aromatic lemony flavour. It looks rather like a long, slender spring onion, but is fibrous and woody and is usually removed before the dish is served. Alternatively, the inner leaves may be very finely sliced, chopped or pounded in a mortar and pestle and used in soups and spice pastes. Dried and powdered lemongrass are also available.

Garlic

1 Put the clove on a chopping board and place the flat side of a large knife on top of it. Press down firmly on the flat of the blade to crush the clove and break the papery skin.

1 Cut off the base of the clove and slip the garlic out of its skin. It should come away easily.

3 Slicing Using a rocking motion with the knife tip on the board, slice the garlic as thinly as you need.

4 Shredding and chopping Holding the slices together, shred them across the slices. Chop the shreds if you need chopped garlic.

5 Crushing After step 2, the whole clove can be put into a garlic press. To crush with a knife: roughly chop the peeled cloves with a pinch of salt. Press down hard with the edge of a large knife tip (with the blade facing away from you), then drag the blade along the garlic while still pressing hard. Continue to do this, dragging the knife tip over the garlic.

Chillies

1 Cut off the cap and slit the chilli open lengthways. Using a spoon, scrape out the seeds and the pith.

2 For diced chilli, cut into thin shreds lengthways, then cut crossways.

Cook's Tip

Wash hands thoroughly after handling chillies – the volatile oils will sting if accidentally rubbed into your eyes.

Spices and sauces

Most spices are sold dried, either whole or ground. For optimum flavour, buy whole spices and grind them yourself.

Spices

Cayenne pepper is made from small, hot dried red chillies. It is always sold ground and is sweet, pungent and very hot. Use it sparingly. Unlike paprika, cayenne pepper cannot be used for colouring as its flavour is too pronounced.

Chilli, available as powder or flakes as well as fresh, is a fiery hot spice and should be used cautiously. Some brands, often called mild chilli powder or chilli seasoning, are a mixture of chilli and other flavourings, such as cumin, oregano, salt and garlic; these are therefore considerably less fiery than hot chilli powder. Adjust the quantity you use accordingly.

Cinnamon is the dried, rolled bark of a tropical evergreen tree. Available as sticks and in powdered form, it has a sweet, pungent flavour. Cinnamon sticks have a more pronounced flavour than the powder, but they are difficult to grind at home, so buy ready-ground cinnamon for use in sweet, spicy baking. Use cinnamon sticks to flavour meat casseroles, vegetable dishes, chutneys and pickles.

Coriander seeds have a mild, sweet, orangey flavour and taste quite different from the fresh green leaves, which are used as a herb. Sold whole or ground, they are an ingredient of most curry powders.

Cumin has a strong, slightly bitter taste, improved by toasting. Sold whole as seeds, or ground, it is an ingredient of curry powders and some chilli powder mixtures.

Curry leaves These shiny leaves have a fresh-tasting flavour akin to curry powder. They are used as a herb in cooking, most often added whole, but sometimes chopped first. The fresh or dried leaves can be used sparingly to flavour soups and stews. Sold fresh in bunches, curry leaves can be frozen in a plastic bag and added to dishes as required.

Fenugreek seeds are yellow-brown and very hard, with a distinctive aroma and slightly harsh, hot flavour. An ingredient of commercial curry powders, fenugreek is also used in chutneys, pickles and sauces.

Nutmeg, seed of the nutmeg fruit, has a distinctive, nutty flavour. Sold whole or ground, but best bought whole since the flavour of freshly grated nutmeg is far superior.

Paprika is a sweet mild spice made from certain varieties of red pepper; it is always sold ground to a red powder. It is good for adding colour to pale egg and cheese dishes. Some varieties, particularly Hungarian, are hotter than others. Paprika doesn't keep its flavour well, so buy little and often. Produced from oak-smoked red peppers, smoked paprika has an intense flavour and wonderful smoky aroma. Sweet, bittersweet and hot-smoked varieties are available.

Saffron, the most expensive of all spices, is the dried stigma of the saffron crocus flower. It has a wonderful subtle flavour and aroma and imparts a hint of yellow to foods it is cooked with. Powdered saffron is available, but it is the whole stigmas, called saffron strands or threads, that give the best results. A generous pinch is all that is needed to flavour and colour dishes.

Turmeric is a member of the ginger family, though it is rarely available fresh. The bright orange root is commonly dried, then ground and sold in powdered form. Turmeric powder has an aromatic, slightly bitter flavour and should be used sparingly in curry powder, pickles, relishes and rice dishes. Like saffron, turmeric colours the foods it is cooked with, but it has a much harsher flavour than saffron.

Thai green curry paste is a blend of spices such as green chillies, coriander and lemongrass. Thai red curry paste contains fresh and dried red chillies and ginger. Once opened, store in a sealed container in the refrigerator.

Sauces

Soy sauce – made from fermented soya beans and, usually, wheat, this is the most common flavouring in Chinese and South-east Asian cooking. There are light and dark soy sauces; the dark kind is slightly sweeter and tends to darken the food. It will keep indefinitely.

Tabasco – a fiery hot sauce based on red chillies, spirit vinegar and salt, and prepared to a secret recipe. A dash of Tabasco may be used to add a kick to soups, casseroles, sauces, rice dishes and tomato-based drinks.

Thai fish sauce – a salty condiment with a distinctive, pungent aroma. It is used in many South-east Asian dishes. You can buy it in most large supermarkets and Asian food stores. It will keep indefinitely.

Coconut milk

Canned coconut milk is widely available, but if you can't find it, use blocks of creamed coconut or coconut powder, following the packet instructions to make the amount of liquid you need.

Which oil to use?

Groundnut (peanut) oil has a mild flavour and is well suited to stir-frying and deep-frying as it has a high smoke point and can therefore be used at high temperatures.
Sesame oil has a distinctive nutty flavour; it is best used in marinades or added as a seasoning to stir-fried dishes just before serving.
Vegetable oil may be pure cold-pressed rapeseed oil, sunflower oil, or a blend of corn, soya bean, rapeseed or other oils. It usually has a bland flavour and is suitable for stir-frying.

Spice mixes

Curry powder - bought curry powders are readily available, but for optimum flavour make your own. **To make your own curry powder:** Put 1 tbsp each cumin and fenugreek seeds, 1/2 tsp mustard seeds, 1 1/2 tsp each poppy seeds, black peppercorns and ground ginger, 4 tbsp coriander seeds, 1/2 tsp hot chilli powder and 2 tbsp ground turmeric into an electric blender or grinder. Grind to a fine powder. Store the curry powder in an airtight container and use within one month.

Garam masala – sold ready-prepared, this Indian spice mix is aromatic rather than hot.
To make your own garam masala: Grind together 10 green cardamom pods, 1 tbsp black peppercorns and 2 tsp cumin seeds. Store in an airtight container and use within one month.

Using herbs

Most herbs are the leaf of a flowering plant, and are usually sold with much of the stalk intact. They have to be washed, trimmed and then chopped or torn into pieces suitable for your recipe.

Washing

1 Trim the roots and part of the stalks from the herbs. Immerse in cold water and shake briskly. Leave in the water for a few minutes.

2 Lift out of the water and put in a colander or sieve, then rinse again under the cold tap. Leave to drain for a few minutes, then dry thoroughly on kitchen paper or teatowels, or use a salad spinner.

Chopping

1 Trim the herbs by pinching off all but the smallest, most tender stalks. If the herb is one with a woody stalk, such as rosemary or thyme, it may be easier to remove the leaves by rubbing the whole bunch between your hands; the leaves should simply pull off the stems.

2 If you are chopping the leaves, gather them into a compact ball in one hand, keeping your fist around the ball (but being careful not to crush them).

3 Chop with a large knife, using a rocking motion and letting just a little of the ball out of your fingers at a time.

4 When the herbs are roughly chopped, continue chopping until the pieces are in small shreds or flakes.

Perfect herbs

- After washing, don't pour the herbs and their water into the sieve, because dirt in the water might get caught in the leaves.
- If the herb has fleshy stalks, such as parsley or coriander, the stalks can be saved to flavour stock or soup. Tie them in a bundle with string for easy removal.

Cooking beans

1 Pick through the beans to remove any grit or stones. Put the beans in a bowl or pan and pour over cold water to cover generously. Leave to soak for at least 8 hours, then drain. (Or pour boiling water over and leave the beans to cool in the water for 1–2 hours.)

2 Put the soaked beans into a large pan and add cold water to cover by at least 5cm (2in). Bring to the boil and boil rapidly for 10 minutes.

3 Skim off the scum that rises to the top, reduce the heat and leave to simmer until the beans are soft inside. They should be tender but not falling apart. Check periodically to make sure there's enough water to keep the beans well covered. Drain well. If using in a salad, allow to cool completely.

Using beans and lentils

Many dried beans and peas need to be soaked overnight before cooking. Lentils do not need soaking and are quicker to cook. Quicker still are canned beans: they are ready to use, but should be drained in a sieve and rinsed in cold water first.

Cooking times

Older beans take longer to cook, so check their 'best before' date. For some pulses, such as red kidney beans, aduki beans, black-eyed beans, black beans and borlotti beans, it is essential to cover them with fresh cold water, bring to the boil and boil rapidly for 10 minutes to destroy any toxins. Then you can reduce the heat and and cook at a steady simmer for the following times:

Chickpeas	1–2 hours
Cannellini, borlotti, butter, flageolet, red kidney beans	1–3 hours
Red lentils	20 minutes
Green lentils	30–40 minutes

Simple Soup Garnishes

Toasted Croûtons

1 Cut the crusts off sliced white bread, then cut into dice 1–2cm (½–¾in) square. Put the bread on a baking sheet and drizzle lightly with oil, then toss well with your hands.

2 Spread the bread dice in a single layer and bake at 200°C (180°C fan oven) mark 6 for 8–10 minutes until lightly browned.

Fried Croûtons

Croûtons fried in a generous amount of oil will crispen all over.

1 Cut the crusts off sliced white bread, then cut into dice 1–2cm (½–¾in) square.

2 Heat the oil medium-hot in a frying pan. Fry in a single layer, stirring constantly, until brown all over. Drain on kitchen paper.

Fresh Herbs

A simple sprinkling of fresh herbs makes a delicious garnish for soups. Fresh herb flowers can also make a pretty and unusual garnish.

1 Chop the herbs just before serving, and choose a herb that complements that flavour of soup – for example, basil with tomato, chives with creamy soups, or coriander with Asian-style soups.

Cream

Cream and other dairy products such as yogurt and crème fraîche can also make a simple garnish, drizzled or spooned on to soup just before serving. They also add body and texture so use sparingly if the soup already includes cream.

Accompaniments

Black Olive Bread

To make 2 loaves, you will need:
2 tsp traditional dried yeast, 500g (1lb 2oz) strong white bread flour, plus extra to dust, 2 tsp coarse salt, plus extra to sprinkle, 6 tbsp extra virgin olive oil, plus extra to grease, 100g (3½oz) black olives, pitted and chopped.

1 Put 150ml (¼ pint) hand-hot water into a jug, stir in the yeast and leave for 10 minutes or until foamy. Put the flour into a bowl or a food processor, then add the salt, yeast mix, 200ml (7fl oz) warm water and 2 tbsp oil. Mix using a wooden spoon or the dough hook for 2–3 minutes to make a soft smooth dough. Put the dough in a lightly oiled bowl; cover with oiled clingfilm and leave in a warm place for 45 minutes or until doubled in size. Punch the dough to knock out the air, then knead on a lightly floured worksurface for 1 minute. Add the olives and knead until combined. Divide in half, shape into rectangles and put into two greased tins, each about 25.5 x 15cm (10 x 6in). Cover with clingfilm and leave in a warm place for 1 hour or until the dough is puffy.

2 Preheat the oven to 200°C (180°C fan oven) mark 6. Press your finger into the dough 12 times, drizzle over 2 tbsp oil and sprinkle with salt. Bake for 30–35 minutes until golden. Drizzle with the remaining oil. Slice and serve warm.

Griddled Garlic Bread

To serve 8, you will need:
175g (6oz) butter, cubed, 3 garlic cloves, crushed, 1 bunch of stiff-stemmed fresh thyme sprigs, 1 large crusty loaf, cut into 2cm (¾in) thick slices, salt and ground black pepper.

1 Preheat a griddle pan. Put the butter and garlic into a pan over a gentle heat and leave to melt. Season with salt and pepper.

2 Dip the thyme into the melted butter and brush one side of each slice of bread. Put the slices, buttered side down, in the griddle pan and cook for 1–2 minutes until crisp and golden. Brush the uppermost sides with the remaining butter, turn over and cook the other side. Serve immediately.

Hygiene

When you are preparing food, always follow these important guidelines:

Wash your hands thoroughly before handling food and again between handling different types of food, such as raw and cooked meat and poultry. If you have any cuts or grazes on your hands, be sure to keep them covered with a waterproof plaster.

Wash down worksurfaces regularly with a mild detergent solution or multi-surface cleaner.

Use a dishwasher if available. Otherwise, wear rubber gloves for washing-up, so that the water temperature can be hotter than unprotected hands can bear. Change drying-up cloths and cleaning cloths regularly. Note that leaving dishes to drain is more hygienic than drying them with a teatowel.

Keep raw and cooked foods separate, especially meat, fish and poultry. Wash kitchen utensils in between preparing raw and cooked foods. Never put cooked or ready-to-eat foods directly on to a surface that has just had raw fish, meat or poultry on it.

Keep pets out of the kitchen if possible; or make sure they stay away from worksurfaces. Never allow animals on to worksurfaces.

Food storage and hygiene

Storing food properly and preparing it in a hygienic way is important to ensure that food remains as nutritious and flavourful as possible, and to reduce the risk of food poisoning.

Shopping

Always choose fresh ingredients in prime condition from stores and markets that have a regular turnover of stock to ensure you buy the freshest produce possible.

Make sure items are within their 'best before' or 'use by' date. (Foods with a longer shelf life have a 'best before' date; more perishable items have a 'use by' date.)

Pack frozen and chilled items in an insulated cool bag at the check-out and put them into the freezer or refrigerator as soon as you get home.

During warm weather in particular, buy perishable foods just before you return home. When packing items at the check-out, sort them according to where you will store them when you get home – the refrigerator, freezer, storecupboard, vegetable rack, fruit bowl, etc. This will make unpacking easier – and quicker.

The storecupboard

Although storecupboard ingredients will generally last a long time, correct storage is important:

Always check packaging for storage advice – even with familiar foods, because storage requirements may change if additives, sugar or salt have been reduced. Check storecupboard foods for their 'best before' or 'use by' date and do not use them if the date has passed.

Keep all food cupboards scrupulously clean and make sure food containers and packets are properly sealed.

Once opened, treat canned foods as though fresh. Always transfer the contents to a clean container, cover and keep in the refrigerator. Similarly, jars, sauce bottles and cartons should be kept chilled after opening. (Check the label for safe storage times after opening.)

Transfer dry goods such as sugar, flour, rice and pasta to moisture-proof containers. When supplies are used up, wash the container well and thoroughly dry before refilling with new supplies.

Store oils in a dark cupboard away from any heat source as heat and light can make them turn rancid and affect their colour. For the same reason, buy olive oil in dark green bottles.

Store vinegars in a cool place; they can turn bad in a warm environment.

Store dried herbs, spices and flavourings in a cool, dark cupboard or in dark jars. Buy in small quantities as their flavour will not last indefinitely.

Refrigerator storage

Fresh food needs to be kept in the cool temperature of the refrigerator to keep it in good condition and discourage the growth of harmful bacteria. Store day-to-day perishable items, such as opened jams and jellies, mayonnaise and bottled sauces, in the refrigerator along with eggs and dairy products, fruit juices, bacon, fresh and cooked meat (on separate shelves), and salads and vegetables (except potatoes, which don't suit being stored in the cold). A refrigerator should be kept at an operating temperature of 4–5°C. It is worth investing in a refrigerator thermometer to ensure the correct temperature is maintained.

To ensure your refrigerator is functioning effectively for safe food storage, follow these guidelines:

To avoid bacterial cross-contamination, store cooked and raw foods on separate shelves, putting cooked foods on the top shelf. Ensure that all items are well wrapped.

Never put hot food into the refrigerator, as this will cause the internal temperature of the refrigerator to rise.

Avoid overfilling the refrigerator, as this restricts the circulation of air and prevents the appliance from working properly.

It can take some time for the refrigerator to return to the correct operating temperature once the door has been opened, so don't leave it open any longer than is necessary.

Clean the refrigerator regularly, using a specially formulated germicidal refrigerator cleaner. Alternatively, use a weak solution of bicarbonate of soda: 1 tbsp to 1 litre (1³/₄ pints) water.

If your refrigerator doesn't have an automatic defrost facility, defrost regularly.

Maximum refrigerator storage times

For pre-packed foods, always adhere to the 'use by' date on the packet. For other foods the following storage times should apply, providing the food is in prime condition when it goes into the refrigerator and that your refrigerator is in good working order:

Vegetables and Fruit

Green vegetables	3–4 days
Salad leaves	2–3 days
Hard and stone fruit	3–7 days
Soft fruit	1–2 days

Dairy Food

Cheese, hard	1 week
Cheese, soft	2–3 days
Eggs	1 week
Milk	4–5 days

Raw Meat

Bacon	7 days
Game	2 days
Minced meat	1 day
Offal	1 day
Poultry	2 days
Raw sliced meat	2 days

Cooked Meat

Sliced meat	2 days
Ham	2 days
Ham, vacuum-packed	1–2 weeks

(or according to the instructions on the packet)

1

Smooth and Creamy

Freezing Tip

To freeze Complete the recipe to the end of step 2, then cool, pack and freeze for up to one month.
To use Thaw the soup overnight at cool room temperature, then complete the recipe.

40g (1½oz) butter

1 onion, roughly chopped

225g (8oz) floury potatoes such as King Edward, peeled and chopped

400g (14oz) parsnips, peeled and chopped

4 tsp paprika, plus extra to dust

1.1 litres (2 pints) vegetable stock

450ml (¾ pint) milk

4 tbsp double cream

75g (3oz) sliced chorizo sausage, cut into fine strips

salt and ground black pepper

parsnip crisps and freshly grated Parmesan to serve

Parsnip Soup with Chorizo

1 Melt the butter in a large heavy-based pan over a gentle heat. Add the onion and cook for 5 minutes until soft. Add the potatoes, parsnips and paprika. Mix well and cook gently, stirring occasionally, for 15 minutes or until the vegetables begin to soften.

2 Add the stock, milk and cream and season with salt and pepper. Bring to the boil, then reduce the heat and simmer for about 25 minutes or until the vegetables are very soft. Add 50g (2oz) chorizo. Leave the soup to cool a little, then whiz in batches in a blender or food processor until smooth. The soup can be thinned with additional stock or milk, if you like. Check the seasoning and put back into the pan.

3 To serve, reheat the soup gently. Ladle into warmed bowls, top each with parsnip crisps, sprinkle with the remaining chorizo and a little Parmesan and dust with paprika.

Serves 8	EASY		NUTRITIONAL INFORMATION	
	Preparation Time 20 minutes	**Cooking Time** 1 hour	**Per Serving** 278 calories, 20g fat (of which 9g saturates), 18g carbohydrate, 0.7g salt	Gluten free

Cook's Tips

Chillies vary enormously in strength, from quite mild to blisteringly hot, depending on the type of chilli and its ripeness. Taste a small piece first to check it's not too hot for you.

Be extremely careful when handling chillies not to touch or rub your eyes with your fingers, as they will sting. Wash knives immediately after handling chillies for the same reason. As a precaution, use rubber gloves when preparing them if you like.

Sweet Potato Soup

1 tbsp olive oil

1 large onion, finely chopped

2 tsp coriander seeds, crushed

2 fresh red chillies, seeded and chopped (see Cook's Tip)

1 butternut squash, about 750g (1lb 10oz), peeled and roughly chopped

2 sweet potatoes, peeled and roughly chopped

2 tomatoes, skinned and diced

1.7 litres (3 pints) hot vegetable stock

cheese straws to serve

1 Heat the oil in a large pan over a gentle heat and fry the onion for about 10 minutes until soft. Add the coriander seeds and chillies to the pan and cook for 1–2 minutes.

2 Add the squash, sweet potatoes and tomatoes and cook for 5 minutes. Add the hot stock, cover and bring to the boil, then reduce the heat and simmer gently for 15 minutes or until the vegetables are soft. Leave the soup to cool a little, then whiz in batches in a blender or food processor until smooth. Reheat gently and serve with a sprinkling of black pepper and cheese straws.

Freezing Tip

To freeze Complete the recipe, then cool, pack and freeze for up to three months.

To use Thaw the soup for 4 hours at cool room temperature. Put in a pan, bring to the boil and simmer for 10 minutes.

EASY		NUTRITIONAL INFORMATION		Serves
Preparation Time 20 minutes	**Cooking Time** 35 minutes	**Per Serving** 78 calories, 2g fat (of which trace saturates), 14g carbohydrate, 0.8g salt	Vegetarian Gluten free • Dairy free	**8**

Leek and Potato Soup

25g (1oz) butter
1 onion, finely chopped
1 garlic clove, crushed
550g (1¼lb) leeks, trimmed and chopped
200g (7oz) floury potatoes, peeled and sliced
1.3 litres (2¼ pints) hot vegetable stock
crème fraîche and chopped chives to garnish

1 Melt the butter in a pan over a gentle heat, then cook the onion for 10–15 minutes until soft. Add the garlic and cook for a further 1 minute. Add the leeks and cook for 5–10 minutes until softened. Add the potatoes and toss together with the leeks.

2 Pour in the hot stock and bring to the boil, then reduce the heat and simmer the soup for 20 minutes until the potatoes are tender.

3 Leave the soup to cool a little, then whiz in batches in a blender or food processor until smooth.

4 To serve, reheat the soup gently. Ladle into warmed bowls and garnish with crème fraîche and chives.

Serves 4	EASY		NUTRITIONAL INFORMATION	
	Preparation Time 10 minutes	**Cooking Time** 45 minutes	**Per Serving** 117 calories, 6g fat (of which 4g saturates), 13g carbohydrate, 0.1g salt	Vegetarian Gluten free

Roasted Tomato and Pepper Soup

1.4kg (3lb) full-flavoured tomatoes, preferably vine-ripened

2 red peppers, cored, seeded and chopped

4 garlic cloves, crushed

3 small onions, thinly sliced

20g (³⁄₄oz) fresh thyme sprigs

4 tbsp olive oil

4 tbsp Worcestershire sauce

4 tbsp vodka

salt and ground black pepper

6 tbsp double cream to serve

1 Preheat the oven to 200°C (180°C fan oven) mark 6. Put the tomatoes into a large roasting tin with the peppers, garlic and onions. Scatter 6 thyme sprigs over the top, drizzle with oil and roast in the oven for 25 minutes. Turn the vegetables over and roast for a further 30–40 minutes until tender and slightly charred.

2 Put one-third of the vegetables into a blender or food processor with 300ml (½ pint) boiled water. Add the Worcestershire sauce and vodka and season with salt and pepper. Whiz until smooth, then pass through a sieve into a pan.

3 Whiz the remaining vegetables with 450ml (³⁄₄ pint) boiled water, then sieve and add to the pan.

4 To serve, warm the soup thoroughly, stirring occasionally. Ladle into warmed bowls, add 1 tbsp double cream to each bowl, then drag a cocktail stick through the cream to swirl. Scatter a few fresh thyme leaves over the top and serve immediately.

EASY		NUTRITIONAL INFORMATION		Serves
Preparation Time 20 minutes	**Cooking Time** about 1 hour	**Per Serving** 239 calories, 16g fat (of which 6g saturates), 15g carbohydrate, 0.4g salt	Gluten free	**6**

Carrot and Coriander Soup

40g (1½ oz) butter
175g (6oz) leeks, trimmed and sliced
450g (1lb) carrots, sliced
2 tsp ground coriander
1 tsp plain flour
1.2 litres (2 pints) vegetable stock
150ml (¼ pint) single cream
salt and ground black pepper
coriander leaves, roughly torn, to serve

1 Melt the butter in a large pan. Add the leeks and carrots, stir, then cover the pan and cook gently for 7–10 minutes until the vegetables begin to soften but not colour.

2 Stir in the ground coriander and flour and cook, stirring, for 1 minute.

3 Add the stock and bring to the boil, stirring. Season with salt and pepper, then reduce the heat, cover the pan and simmer for about 20 minutes, until the vegetables are tender.

4 Leave the soup to cool a little, then whiz in batches in a blender or food processor until quite smooth. Return to the pan and stir in the cream. Adjust the seasoning and reheat gently; do not boil.

5 Ladle into warmed bowls, scatter with torn coriander leaves and serve.

EASY		NUTRITIONAL INFORMATION		Serves
Preparation Time 15 minutes	**Cooking Time** about 30 minutes	**Per Serving** 140 calories, 11g fat (of which 7g saturates), 10g carbohydrate, 0.2g salt	Vegetarian Gluten free	6

Mixed Mushroom Soup

15g (½ oz) dried porcini mushrooms

1 tbsp sunflower oil, plus 50ml (2fl oz) to shallow-fry

1 small onion, chopped

450g (1lb) chestnut mushrooms, chopped

600ml (1 pint) hot vegetable stock

2 slices white bread, crusts removed, cut into cubes

2 garlic cloves, finely sliced

salt and ground black pepper

freshly chopped flat-leafed parsley to garnish

1 Put the porcini into a bowl, pour 75ml (2½fl oz) boiling water over them and leave to soak for 10 minutes. Strain the porcini, put the liquid to one side, then chop roughly, keeping 1 tbsp for a garnish.

2 Heat 1 tbsp oil in a pan. Add the onion and porcini and cook over a medium heat for 5 minutes. Add the chestnut mushrooms, increase the heat and brown lightly for 5 minutes. Add the reserved porcini liquid and the stock, then bring to the boil. Season well with salt and pepper, reduce the heat and simmer for 20 minutes.

3 To make croûtons, heat 50ml (2fl oz) oil in a frying pan. Add the bread and garlic and stir-fry for 2 minutes until golden. Drain on kitchen paper.

4 Take the soup off the heat and leave to cool a little. Whiz in a blender or food processor until smooth, then transfer to a clean pan. Reheat gently, then ladle into warmed bowls and serve topped with the croûtons, reserved porcini and a sprinkling of parsley.

Serves 4	EASY		NUTRITIONAL INFORMATION	
	Preparation Time 15 minutes, plus soaking	**Cooking Time** 35 minutes	**Per Serving** 158 calories, 12g fat (of which 2g saturates), 10g carbohydrate, 0.2g salt	Dairy free

Courgette and Leek Soup

1 tbsp olive oil
1 onion, finely chopped
2 leeks, trimmed and sliced
900g (2lb) courgettes, grated
1.3 litres (2³/₄ pints) hot vegetable or chicken stock
4 short rosemary sprigs
1 small baguette
125g (4oz) grated Gruyère cheese
salt and ground black pepper

1 Heat the oil in a large pan. Add the onion and leeks and cook for 5–10 minutes. Add the courgettes and cook, stirring, for a further 5 minutes.

2 Add the hot stock and 3 rosemary sprigs, then bring to the boil. Season with salt and pepper, reduce the heat and simmer for 20 minutes.

3 Preheat the grill to medium-high. Slice the bread diagonally into eight and grill for 1–2 minutes on one side until golden. Turn the bread over, sprinkle with the cheese and season. Grill for a further 1–2 minutes. Keep the croûtes warm.

4 Leave the soup to cool a little. Remove the rosemary stalks and whiz the soup in batches in a blender or food processor until smooth. Pour into a clean pan and reheat gently.

5 Ladle into warmed bowls, garnish with the croûtes and sprinkle with the remaining rosemary leaves.

EASY		**NUTRITIONAL INFORMATION**		Serves
Preparation Time 15 minutes	**Cooking Time** 35–40 minutes	**Per Serving** 246 calories, 9g fat (of which 3g saturates), 32g carbohydrate, 1g salt	Vegetarian	**8**

Cook's Tips

Melba Toast: cut 4–5 thin slices from a day-old loaf of wholemeal bread. Toast lightly on both sides. Quickly cut off the crusts and split each slice in two horizontally. Bake in a 180°C (160°C fan) mark 4 oven for 10–15 minutes until crisp and curled.
For a less rich soup, use semi-skimmed milk rather than single cream.

Cream of Jerusalem Artichoke Soup

450g (1lb) Jerusalem artichokes
50g (2oz) butter
2 shallots, diced
1 tsp mild curry paste
900ml (1½ pints) vegetable stock
150ml (¼ pint) single cream
freshly grated nutmeg to taste
pinch of cayenne pepper
4 tbsp freshly grated Parmesan
salt and ground black pepper
3–4 slices hot Melba toast to serve (see Cook's Tips)

1 Scrub the Jerusalem artichokes thoroughly, pat dry, then slice thinly.

2 Melt the butter in a large pan, add the shallots and cook gently for 10 minutes until soft and golden.

3 Stir in the curry paste and cook for 1 minute. Add the sliced artichokes and stock and stir well, then bring to the boil. Reduce the heat, cover the pan and simmer for about 15 minutes until the artichokes are tender.

4 Add the cream, nutmeg and cayenne to the soup. Transfer to a blender or food processor and whiz until smooth, then pass through a sieve into a clean pan.

5 Reheat the soup gently and stir in the grated Parmesan. Taste and adjust the seasoning. Ladle into warmed bowls and serve at once, with the Melba toast.

Serves 6	EASY		NUTRITIONAL INFORMATION	
	Preparation Time 15 minutes	**Cooking Time** 30 minutes	**Per Serving** 220 calories, 17g fat (of which 10.5g saturates), 9g carbohydrate, 1g salt	Vegetarian

SMOOTH AND CREAMY   **41**

Cook's Tip

Serve this smooth, rich soup with warmed bridge rolls, before a main course of plain roast or grilled meat.

1 small baguette, thinly sliced

2 tbsp basil-infused olive oil, plus extra to drizzle

450g (1lb) frozen peas, thawed

600ml (1 pint) vegetable stock

salt and ground black pepper

Easy Pea Soup

1 Preheat the oven to 220°C (200°C fan oven) mark 7. To make the croûtons, put the bread on a baking sheet, drizzle with 2 tbsp oil and bake for 10–15 minutes until golden.

2 Meanwhile, put the peas in a food processor, add the stock and season with salt and pepper. Whiz for 2–3 minutes.

3 Pour the soup into a pan and bring to the boil, then reduce the heat and simmer for 10 minutes. Spoon into warmed bowls, add the croûtons, drizzle with extra oil and sprinkle with salt and pepper. Serve immediately.

EASY		NUTRITIONAL INFORMATION		Serves
Preparation Time 2 minutes, plus thawing	**Cooking Time** 15 minutes	**Per Serving** 408 calories, 9g fat (of which 2g saturates), 69g carbohydrate, 1.8g salt	Vegetarian • Dairy free	**4**

Turkey and Chestnut Soup

25g (1oz) butter or margarine

1 large onion, chopped

225g (8oz) Brussels sprouts

900ml (1½ pints) turkey stock made from leftover carcass and any leftover turkey meat

400g can whole chestnuts, drained

2 tsp freshly chopped thyme or 1 tsp dried thyme

salt and ground black pepper

stock or milk to finish

thyme sprigs to garnish

1 Melt the fat in a large heavy-based saucepan, add the onion and fry gently for 5 minutes until it has softened.

2 Trim the sprouts and cut a cross in the base of each one. Add to the onion, cover the pan with a lid and cook gently for 5 minutes, shaking the pan frequently.

3 Pour in the stock and bring to the boil, then add the remaining ingredients, with salt and pepper to taste. Reduce the heat, cover the pan and simmer for 30 minutes until the vegetables are tender.

4 Leave the soup to cool a little, then whiz in batches in a blender or food processor until smooth. Return to the rinsed-out pan and reheat gently, then thin down with either stock or milk, according to taste.

5 Taste and adjust the seasoning. To serve, ladle into warmed bowls and garnish with sprigs of thyme.

Cook's Tip

Serve for an informal family lunch with hot garlic bread, wholemeal toast, cheese on toast or hot sausage rolls.

EASY		NUTRITIONAL INFORMATION		Serves
Preparation Time 5 minutes	**Cooking Time** 45 minutes	**Per Serving** 330 calories, 10g fat (of which 4.5g saturates), 52g carbohydrate, 0.2g salt	Gluten free	**4**

Try Something Different

Double the quantity of goat's cheese if you prefer a stronger taste.
Instead of goat's cheese, substitute a soft garlic cheese for a really garlicky flavour.

Broccoli and Goat's Cheese Soup

50g (2oz) butter

2 medium onions, chopped

1 litre (1³/₄ pints) vegetable, chicken or turkey stock

700g (1¹/₂lb) broccoli, broken into florets, stout stalks peeled and chopped

1 head of garlic, separated into cloves

1 tbsp olive oil

150g (5oz) goat's cheese

salt and ground black pepper

1 Preheat the oven to 200°C (180°C fan oven) mark 6. Melt the butter in a saucepan over a gentle heat. Add the onions, then cover the pan and cook for 4–5 minutes until translucent. Add half the stock and bring to the boil. Add the broccoli and return to the boil, then cover the pan, reduce the heat and simmer for 15–20 minutes or until the broccoli is tender.

2 Toss the cloves of garlic in the oil and tip into a roasting tin. Roast in the oven for 15 minutes until soft when squeezed.

3 Leave the soup to cool a little, then add the goat's cheese and whiz in batches in a blender or food processor until smooth. Return the soup to the pan and add the remaining stock. Reheat gently on the hob and season to taste with salt and pepper.

4 Ladle the soup into warmed bowls, squeeze the garlic out of their skins and scatter over the soup, add a sprinkling of black pepper and serve.

Serves 6	EASY		NUTRITIONAL INFORMATION	
	Preparation Time 10 minutes	**Cooking Time** 20 minutes	**Per Serving** 220 calories, 16g fat (of which 9.5g saturates), 7.6g carbohydrate, 0.5g salt	Vegetarian Gluten free

Cook's Tip

Serve this smooth, rich soup with warmed bridge rolls, before a main course of plain roast or grilled meat.

3 tbsp plain flour

150ml (¼ pint) milk

1.1 litres (2 pints) homemade chicken stock

125g (4oz) cooked chicken, diced

1 tsp lemon juice

a pinch of freshly grated nutmeg

2 tbsp single cream

salt and ground black pepper

croûtons and parsley sprigs to garnish

Cream of Chicken Soup

1 Put the flour into a large bowl, add a little of the milk and blend until it makes a smooth cream.

2 Bring the stock to the boil, then stir it into the blended mixture. Return to the pan and simmer gently for 20 minutes.

3 Stir in the chicken, lemon juice and nutmeg and season to taste with salt and pepper. Mix the rest of the milk with the cream and stir in, then reheat without boiling.

4 Taste and adjust the seasoning. Ladle the soup into warmed bowls, sprinkle with croûtons and parsley sprigs and serve.

EASY		NUTRITIONAL INFORMATION		Serves
Preparation Time 10 minutes	**Cooking Time** 30 minutes	**Per Serving** 398 calories, 12g fat (of which 6g saturates), 44g carbohydrate, 0.5g salt	Gluten free	**4**

Cook's Tip

To make the Parmesan crisps, preheat the oven to 200°C (180°C fan oven) mark 6 and line two baking sheets with baking parchment. Put heaped tablespoons of Parmesan on the sheets, spacing them well apart, and spread each one out. Sprinkle with poppy seeds and bake for 5–10 minutes until lacy golden. Leave on the baking sheet for 2–3 minutes to firm up slightly, then transfer to a wire rack to cool.

Creamy Watercress Soup

250g (9oz) watercress

50g (2oz) butter

1 onion, finely chopped

700g (1½lb) potatoes, peeled and cut into small pieces

900ml (1½ pints) milk

900ml (1½ pints) vegetable stock

6 tbsp single cream

salt and ground black pepper

Parmesan Crisps (see Cook's Tip) to serve (optional)

1   Trim the watercress and discard coarse stalks. Reserve a few sprigs of watercress to garnish, then roughly chop the rest.

2   Melt the butter in a large pan, add the onion and cook gently for 8–10 minutes until soft. Add the potatoes and cook for 1 minute, then pour in the milk and stock and bring to the boil. Reduce the heat and simmer for 15–20 minutes until tender.

3   Take the pan off the heat. Stir in the chopped watercress, then transfer to a blender and blend, in batches, until smooth. Pour the soup into a clean pan, then add the cream and season with salt and pepper. Heat through, then serve garnished with the reserved watercress sprigs, with the Parmesan crisps on the side.

Serves 6	EASY		NUTRITIONAL INFORMATION	
	Preparation Time 15 minutes	**Cooking Time** 30 minutes	**Per Serving** 251 calories, 13g fat (of which 8g saturates), 26g carbohydrate, 0.4g salt	Vegetarian Gluten free

Freezing Tip

To freeze Complete the recipe to the end of step 2, then cool half or all the soup, pack and freeze for up to three months.

To use Thaw the soup overnight at cool room temperature. Reheat gently and simmer over a low heat for 5 minutes.

Beetroot Soup

1 tbsp olive oil

1 onion, finely chopped

750g (1lb 10oz) raw beetroot, peeled and cut into 1cm (½in) cubes

275g (10oz) potatoes, peeled and roughly chopped

2 litres (3½ pints) hot vegetable stock

juice of 1 lemon

4 tbsp soured cream

25g (1oz) mixed root vegetable crisps

salt and ground black pepper

2 tbsp chopped chives to garnish

1 Heat the oil in a large pan, add the onion and cook for 5 minutes. Add the vegetables and cook for a further 5 minutes.

2 Add the hot stock and lemon juice, then bring to the boil. Season with salt and pepper, reduce the heat and simmer, half-covered, for 25 minutes. Leave the soup to cool a little, then whiz in batches in a blender or food processor until smooth.

3 Cool half the soup, then freeze it. Pour the remainder into a clean pan and reheat gently. Ladle into warmed bowls, add 1 tbsp soured cream to each bowl, top with a few vegetable crisps and sprinkle the chopped chives on top to serve.

EASY		NUTRITIONAL INFORMATION		Serves
Preparation Time 15 minutes	**Cooking Time** 40–45 minutes	**Per Serving** 216 calories, 9g fat (of which 3g saturates), 31g carbohydrate, 1.5g salt	Vegetarian Gluten free	**8**

Creamed Celeriac and Parmesan Soup

2 tbsp sunflower oil

175g (6oz) onions, roughly chopped

1 garlic clove, crushed

450g (1lb) each celeriac and potatoes, peeled and roughly chopped

1.1 litres (2 pints) vegetable stock

1 bouquet garni (see page 59)

600ml (1 pint) full-fat milk

284ml carton double cream

1 tbsp lemon juice

8 tbsp freshly grated Parmesan

Toasted Parmesan to serve (see Cook's Tip)

1 Heat the oil in a large pan, then add the onions and garlic. Cook slowly for 4–5 minutes or until golden brown.

2 Add the celeriac, potatoes, stock and bouquet garni and bring to the boil, then reduce the heat and simmer for 20–25 minutes or until the celeriac and potatoes are tender.

3 Leave the soup to cool a little, then discard the bouquet garni. Whiz the soup in batches in a blender or food processor until smooth. Pour into a clean pan, add the milk, cream and lemon juice and season with salt and pepper. Simmer for a further 10 minutes.

4 To serve, put 1 tbsp grated Parmesan in the bottom of each warmed serving bowl. Ladle in the soup, grind over some black pepper and garnish with the Toasted Parmesan.

Cook's Tip

Toasted Parmesan: sprinkle 25g (1oz) finely grated Parmesan on to a baking sheet. Put under a hot grill until melted and golden. Cool, then crumble and store in an airtight container for up to one week.

Serves 8	EASY		NUTRITIONAL INFORMATION	
	Preparation Time 10 minutes	**Cooking Time** 35 minutes	**Per Serving** 357 calories, 29g fat (of which 15.4g saturates), 20g carbohydrate, 0.5g salt	Vegetarian Gluten free

Pumpkin and Butternut Squash Soup

900g (2lb) pumpkin, peeled and roughly diced
750g (1lb 10oz) butternut squash, peeled and roughly diced
125g (4oz) shallots, roughly chopped
1 fat garlic clove, chopped
1 tsp coriander seeds, crushed
125g (4oz) butter, melted
600ml (1 pint) vegetable stock
600ml (1 pint) full-fat milk
salt and ground black pepper
basil sprigs and soured cream to garnish
crusty bread or small Yorkshire puddings to serve

1 Preheat the oven to 220°C (200°C fan oven) mark 7. Put the pumpkin, squash, shallots, garlic and coriander seeds into a large roasting tin and toss with the melted butter. Season the vegetables well with salt and pepper and bake for about 30 minutes until golden and just cooked through.

2 Meanwhile, in separate pans, heat the stock and milk.

3 Transfer the vegetables to a large pan, then pour the hot stock into the roasting tin and stir to loosen the remaining bits in the tin. Add this to the vegetables in the pan, then stir in the milk.

4 Put three-quarters of the soup into a blender or food processor and whiz until smooth. Mash the remaining soup mixture, then stir the two together and reheat gently. Ladle into warmed bowls, garnish with basil and swirls of soured cream, then serve with crusty bread or small Yorkshire puddings.

Serves 4	EASY		NUTRITIONAL INFORMATION	
	Preparation Time 20 minutes	**Cooking Time** 40 minutes	**Per Serving** 398 calories, 32.5g fat (of which 21g saturates), 19g carbohydrate, 0.8g salt	Vegetarian Gluten free

Kale and Leek Soup

450g (1lb) leeks, trimmed

25g (1oz) butter

2 rashers streaky bacon, rinded and chopped

450g (1lb) kale, washed and chopped

900ml (1½ pints) chicken stock

2 tbsp freshly chopped parsley

½ tsp freshly chopped tarragon

2 tbsp cornflour

150ml (¼ pint) milk

salt and ground black pepper

1 Slice the leeks, place in a colander or sieve and wash thoroughly. Drain.

2 Melt the butter in a pan, add the leeks and bacon and cook for 5 minutes. Remove from the pan and set aside. Add the kale to the pan and cook for 5 minutes.

3 Return the leeks and bacon to the pan with the stock and herbs and season to taste with salt and pepper. Cover the pan and bring to the boil, then reduce the heat and simmer gently for 35–40 minutes.

4 Leave the soup to cool a little, then whiz in batches in a blender or food processor until smooth.

5 Return the soup to a clean pan. Blend the cornflour to a smooth paste with the milk. Add to the pan, reheat gently until hot, stirring, and cook for 2 minutes. Ladle into warmed bowls and serve.

EASY		NUTRITIONAL INFORMATION		Serves
Preparation Time 10 minutes	**Cooking Time** 55 minutes	**Per Serving** 131 calories, 8g fat (of which 4g saturates), 9g carbohydrate, 0.3g salt	Gluten free	**6**

2

Meal in a Bowl

Fast Fish Soup

1 leek, trimmed and finely chopped

4 fat garlic cloves, crushed

3 celery sticks, finely chopped

1 small fennel bulb, finely chopped

1 red chilli, seeded and finely chopped (see page 33)

3 tbsp olive oil

50ml (2fl oz) dry white wine

about 750g (1lb 11oz) mixed fish and shellfish, such as haddock and monkfish fillets, peeled and deveined raw prawns, and fresh mussels, scrubbed and cleaned (discard any mussels that don't close when tapped on a worksurface or that have broken shells)

4 tomatoes, chopped

20g (³/₄oz) freshly chopped thyme

salt and ground black pepper

1 Put the leek into a large pan and add the garlic, celery, fennel, chilli and oil. Cook over a medium heat for 5 minutes or until the vegetables are soft and beginning to colour.

2 Stir in 1.1 litres (2 pints) boiling water and the wine. Bring to the boil, then reduce the heat, cover the pan and simmer for 5 minutes.

3 Cut the white fish into large chunks. Add to the soup with the tomatoes and thyme. Continue to simmer gently until the fish has just turned opaque. Add the prawns, simmer for 1 minute, then add the mussels, if you're using them.

4 As soon as all the mussels have opened (discard any that do not), season the soup with salt and pepper. Ladle into warmed bowls and serve immediately.

Try Something Different

To give the soup more of a kick, stir in 2 tbsp Pernod instead of the wine.

Garlic croûtes are traditionally served with fish soup; they can be made while the soup is simmering. Toast small slices of baguette, spread with garlic mayonnaise and sprinkle with grated cheese. Float in the hot soup just before serving.

EASY		NUTRITIONAL INFORMATION		Serves
Preparation Time 10 minutes	**Cooking Time** about 15 minutes	**Per Serving** 269 calories, 10g fat (of which 2g saturates), 6g carbohydrate, 0.4g salt	Gluten free • Dairy free	**4**

175g (6oz) podded broad beans

25g (1oz) butter

2 tbsp sunflower oil

1 onion, sliced

225g (8oz) baby carrots, trimmed and halved

225g (8oz) courgettes, cut into 2cm (³/₄in) chunks

1 garlic clove, crushed

1.1kg (2¹/₂lb) thick cod fillet, skinned

4 tbsp plain flour

150ml (¹/₄ pint) dry white wine

300ml (¹/₂ pint) fish stock

1 tbsp lemon juice

3 tbsp double cream

2 tbsp freshly chopped flat-leafed parsley

salt and ground black pepper

baby new potatoes to serve (optional)

Navarin of Cod Soup

1 If the beans are large, blanch them in boiling water for 1–2 minutes, then drain and refresh in cold water.

2 Heat half the butter and half the oil in a large sauté pan. Add the onion, carrots, courgettes and garlic and cook gently until softened and just beginning to brown. Remove from the pan and put to one side.

3 Season the fish with salt and pepper, then dust lightly with the flour. Heat the remaining butter and oil in the pan, add the fish and brown on all sides. Remove from the pan and put to one side.

4 Add the wine to the pan, scraping up any sediment from the bottom. Simmer for 1–2 minutes, then put the carrot mixture and fish back in the pan. Add the beans and stock. Bring to a simmer, cover and simmer gently for about 10 minutes until the fish is opaque and flakes easily. Stir in the lemon juice, cream and parsley. Ladle into warmed bowls and serve with baby new potatoes, if you like.

Serves 6	EASY		NUTRITIONAL INFORMATION
	Preparation Time 15 minutes	**Cooking Time** 25 minutes	**Per Serving** 346 calories, 13g fat (of which 5g saturates), 16g carbohydrate, 0.4g salt

Smoked Cod and Sweetcorn Chowder

130g pack cubed pancetta
50g (2oz) butter
3 leeks, about 450g (1lb), trimmed and thinly sliced
25g (1oz) plain flour
600ml (1 pint) semi-skimmed or full-fat milk
700g (1½lb) undyed smoked cod loin or haddock, skinned and cut into 2cm (¾in) cubes
326g can sweetcorn in water, drained
450g (1lb) small new potatoes, scrubbed and sliced
150ml (¼ pint) double cream
½ tsp paprika
salt and ground black pepper
2 tbsp freshly chopped flat-leafed parsley to garnish

1 Fry the pancetta in a large pan over a gentle heat until the fat runs out. Add the butter to the pan to melt, then add the leeks and cook until softened.

2 Stir in the flour and cook for a few seconds, then pour in the milk and 300ml (½ pint) cold water. Add the fish to the pan with the sweetcorn and potatoes. Bring to the boil, then reduce the heat and simmer for 10–15 minutes until the potatoes are cooked.

3 Stir in the cream, season to taste with salt and pepper and the paprika and cook for 2–3 minutes to warm through. Ladle into warmed shallow bowls and sprinkle each one with a little chopped parsley. Serve immediately.

EASY		NUTRITIONAL INFORMATION	Serves
Preparation Time 5 minutes	**Cooking Time** 20 minutes	**Per Serving** 517 calories, 28g fat (of which 15g saturates), 35g carbohydrate, 4.7g salt	**6**

Freezing Tip

To freeze Complete the soup to the end of step 2, then cool quickly, pack and freeze for up to one month.
To use Thaw the soup overnight at cool room temperature, then complete the recipe.

Squash, Lentil and Prawn Soup

75g (3oz) butter

75g (3oz) each carrots, onions, celery and leeks, roughly chopped

2 garlic cloves, crushed

175g (6oz) Puy lentils

900ml (1½ pints) fish stock

200ml (7fl oz) vermouth

140ml (4½ fl oz) double cream

2 fresh thyme sprigs

2 bay leaves

6–8 small squashes, each weighing about 700g (1lb 9oz)

18–24 large raw prawns, peeled and deveined

salt and ground black pepper

chopped chives to garnish

1 Heat 50g (2oz) butter in a large pan and cook the vegetables, stirring occasionally, for 5 minutes. Add the garlic and cook for 1 minute. Stir in the lentils, stock and 150ml (¼ pint) vermouth with the cream, herbs and seasoning. Add 300ml (½ pint) water. Bring to the boil, cover and simmer for 40–45 minutes until the vegetables are tender. Discard the herbs.

2 Meanwhile, preheat the oven to 200°C (180°C fan oven) mark 6. Trim the bases of the squashes so that they are flat, and cut the tops off at the stalk end. Scoop out the seeds. Put the squashes in a roasting tin and cook for 40 minutes or until tender. Scoop out some of the flesh and add to the soup. Leave the soup to cool a little, then whiz in batches in a blender or food processor until smooth. Pass through a fine sieve, if you like, and adjust the seasoning. If the soup is too thick, dilute with stock or water, put back into the wiped-out pan and keep warm.

3 Put the prawns into a pan with the remaining butter and vermouth and simmer for 2–3 minutes until the prawns turn pink. Strain the prawn liquid into the soup. Ladle into warmed bowls or the hollowed-out squashes, add the prawns and garnish with the chives.

Serves 6	EASY		NUTRITIONAL INFORMATION	
	Preparation Time 20 minutes	**Cooking Time** 55 minutes	**Per Serving** 388 calories, 24g fat (of which 15g saturates), 21g carbohydrate, 0.7g salt	Gluten free

Cook's Tip

To make a bouquet garni, tie together a sprig each of thyme and parsley with a bay leaf and a piece of celery.

75g (3oz) butter

700g (1½lb) small onions, finely chopped

3 garlic cloves, crushed

1 tbsp plain flour

200ml (7fl oz) dry white wine

1.5 litres (2½ pints) vegetable stock

1 bouquet garni (see Cook's Tip)

salt and ground black pepper

1 small baguette, cut into slices
1cm (½in) thick, to serve

50g (2oz) Gruyère cheese or Cheddar, grated, to serve

French Onion Soup

1 Melt the butter in a large heavy-based pan. Add the onions and cook slowly over a very low heat, stirring frequently, until very soft and golden brown; this should take at least 30 minutes. Add the garlic and flour and cook, stirring, for 1 minute. Pour in the wine and let bubble until reduced by half. Add the stock, bouquet garni and seasoning. Bring to the boil, then reduce the heat and simmer gently, uncovered, for 20–30 minutes.

2 Discard the bouquet garni. Leave the soup to cool a little. Put one-third into a blender or food processor, whiz until smooth, then stir back into the soup in the pan.

3 Preheat the grill. Lightly toast the slices of French bread on both sides. Reheat the soup and adjust the seasoning. Divide the soup among four ovenproof soup bowls. Float two or three slices of toast on each portion and sprinkle thickly with the grated cheese. Stand the bowls under the hot grill until the cheese has melted and turned golden brown. Serve at once.

EASY		NUTRITIONAL INFORMATION	Serves
Preparation Time 30 minutes	**Cooking Time** about 1 hour	**Per Serving** 438 calories, 21g fat (of which 13g saturates), 45g carbohydrate, 1.3g salt	**4**

Quick Winter Minestrone

2 tbsp olive oil

1 small onion, finely chopped

1 carrot, chopped

1 celery stick, chopped

1 garlic clove, crushed

2 tbsp freshly chopped thyme

1 litre (1¾ pints) vegetable stock

400g can chopped tomatoes

400g can borlotti beans, drained and rinsed

125g (4oz) minestrone pasta

175g (6oz) Savoy cabbage, shredded

salt and ground black pepper

fresh ready-made pesto (see page 67), toasted ciabatta and extra virgin olive oil to serve

1 Heat the olive oil in a large pan and add the onion, carrot and celery. Cook for 8–10 minutes until softened, then add the garlic and thyme. Fry for another 2–3 minutes.

2 Add the stock, tomatoes and half the borlotti beans. Mash the remaining beans, stir into the soup and simmer for 30 minutes, adding the minestrone pasta and cabbage for the last 10 minutes of cooking time.

3 Check the seasoning and correct, if necessary. Ladle into warmed bowls and serve with a dollop of fresh pesto on top and slices of toasted ciabatta drizzled with extra virgin olive oil on the side.

Serves	EASY		NUTRITIONAL INFORMATION	
4	**Preparation Time** 10 minutes	**Cooking Time** 45 minutes	**Per Serving** 334 calories, 11g fat (of which 3g saturates), 47g carbohydrate, 1.5g salt	Dairy free

Turkey, Ham and Spinach Broth

125g (4oz) green or yellow split peas, soaked overnight in double their volume of cold water

25g (1oz) butter

225g (8oz) onions, chopped

1 tbsp ground coriander

40g (1½oz) pearl barley

2 litres (3½ pints) ham or turkey stock

1 bouquet garni (see page 59)

225g (8oz) potatoes, peeled and cut into chunks

400g (14oz) carrots, cut into chunks

150g (5oz) each cooked turkey and ham, cut into chunks

150g (5oz) baby spinach leaves

salt and ground black pepper

coriander sprigs and black pepper to garnish

50g (2oz) finely grated Parmesan to serve (optional)

1 Drain the split peas, put into a pan and cover with cold water. Bring to the boil, then reduce the heat and simmer for 10 minutes. Drain the peas and discard the liquid.

2 Meanwhile, melt the butter in a pan, add the onions and cook for 5 minutes or until soft but not coloured. Add the ground coriander and cook for 30 seconds.

3 Add the split peas, pearl barley and stock to the pan. Tie the bay leaf, celery and thyme sprig together and add to the pan. Bring to the boil, then reduce the heat and simmer for 40 minutes or until the peas and barley are tender. Add the potatoes and cook for 5 minutes, then add the carrots and cook for 5–10 minutes. Season to taste with salt and pepper.

4 Add the turkey, ham and spinach to the pan and bring back to the boil, then reduce the heat and simmer for 2–3 minutes. Ladle into warmed bowls, garnish with coriander sprigs and pepper and serve with grated Parmesan, if you like.

EASY		NUTRITIONAL INFORMATION		Serves
Preparation Time 20 minutes, plus soaking	**Cooking Time** 1¼ hours	**Per Serving** 243 calories, 5.5g fat (of which 2.8g saturates), 32g carbohydrate, 1g salt	Dairy free	**6**

Scotch Broth

1 piece of marrow bone, about 350g (12oz)

1.4kg (3lb) piece of beef skirt (ask your butcher for this)

300ml (½ pint) broth mix (to include pearl barley, red lentils, split peas and green peas), soaked according to the packet instructions

2 carrots, finely chopped

1 parsnip, finely chopped

2 onions, finely chopped

¼ white cabbage, finely chopped

1 leek, trimmed and finely chopped

1–2 tbsp salt

ground black pepper

2 tbsp freshly chopped parsley to serve

1 Put the marrow bone and beef skirt into a 5.7 litre (10 pint) stock pot and add 2.6 litres (4½ pints) cold water – there should be enough to cover the meat.

2 Bring the water to the boil. Remove any scum from the surface with a spoon and discard. Reduce the heat to low, add the broth mix and simmer, partially covered, for 1½ hours, skimming the surface occasionally.

3 Add the carrots, parsnip, onions, cabbage, leek and another 600ml (1 pint) cold water. Cover to bring to the boil quickly, then reduce the heat and simmer for 30 minutes.

4 Remove the marrow bone and piece of beef from the broth. Add a few shreds of beef to the broth if you like. Season the broth well with the salt and some pepper and stir in the chopped parsley. Ladle into warmed bowls and serve hot.

Cook's Tip

This is really two meals in one, a starter and a main course. The beef flavours the stock and is removed before serving. Later you divide up the meat and serve it with mashed potatoes, swedes or turnips.

Serves	EASY		NUTRITIONAL INFORMATION	
8	**Preparation Time** 15 minutes	**Cooking Time** 2 hours	**Per Serving** 173 calories, 2g fat (of which trace saturates), 35g carbohydrate, 2.3g salt	Dairy free

Cook's Tip

Dried peas form the base of this comforting soup. First, you need to soak them overnight in about 1 litre (1¾ pints) cold water. If you forget, put them straight into a pan with the water, bring to the boil and cook for 1–2 minutes, then leave to stand for 2 hours before using.

Split Pea and Ham Soup

500g pack dried yellow split peas, soaked overnight (see Cook's Tip)

25g (1oz) butter

1 large onion, finely chopped

125g (4oz) rindless smoked streaky bacon rashers, roughly chopped

1 garlic clove, crushed

1.7 litres (3 pints) well-flavoured ham or vegetable stock

1 bouquet garni (see page 59)

1 tsp dried oregano

salt and ground black pepper

125g (4oz) cooked ham, chopped

cracked black pepper to serve

1 Drain the soaked split peas. Melt the butter in a large pan, add the onion, bacon and garlic and cook over a low heat for about 10 minutes until the onion is soft.

2 Add the drained split peas to the pan with the stock. Bring to the boil and skim the surface. Add the bouquet garni and oregano, then season with salt and pepper. Reduce the heat, cover the pan and simmer for 45 minutes to 1 hour or until the peas are very soft.

3 Cool a little, then whiz half the soup in a blender or food processor until smooth. Return to the pan and reheat, then add the ham and check the seasoning. Ladle into warmed bowls and sprinkle with cracked black pepper to serve.

Serves 6	EASY		NUTRITIONAL INFORMATION	
	Preparation Time 15 minutes, plus overnight soaking	**Cooking Time** 1 hour 5 minutes	**Per Serving** 400 calories, 10g fat (of which 4.5g saturates), 52.5g carbohydrate, 1.5g salt	Gluten free

50g (2oz) butter

1 medium onion, diced

450g (1lb) potatoes, peeled and diced

100g (3¹/₂oz) diced bacon

1 garlic clove, chopped

100g (3¹/₂oz) white of leek, chopped

2 Cox Orange Pippins apples, unpeeled, cored and chopped

2 tsp dried thyme

1 tsp dill seeds (optional)

salt and ground black pepper

600ml (1 pint) dry cider

900ml (1¹/₂ pints) hot vegetable stock

125g (4oz) Savoy cabbage leaves, shredded

Autumn Vegetable Soup

1 Melt the butter in a large pan, then add the onion, potatoes, bacon, garlic, leek, apple, thyme and dill, if using. Season to taste with salt and pepper, stir, then cover the pan and cook gently for 15 minutes.

2 Add the cider and bring to the boil, then reduce the heat and simmer for 5 minutes. Add the hot stock and simmer for about 15 minutes until the potatoes are soft.

3 Pour half the soup into a blender or liquidiser and whiz until smooth, then add to the remaining soup in the pan. Reheat gently, add the shredded cabbage and simmer for a further 3 minutes. Ladle into warmed bowls and serve.

EASY		NUTRITIONAL INFORMATION	Serves
Preparation Time 15 minutes	**Cooking Time** 45 minutes	**Per Serving** 326 calories, 16.7g fat (of which 9g saturates), 28.5g carbohydrate, 1.1g salt	**4**

1 oven-ready chicken, about 1.4kg (3lb)

2 onions, roughly chopped

2 carrots, roughly chopped

2 celery sticks, roughly chopped

1 bay leaf

25g (1oz) butter

900g (2lb) leeks, trimmed and sliced

125g (4oz) ready-to-eat stoned prunes, sliced

salt and ground black pepper

freshly chopped parsley to serve

For the dumplings

125g (4oz) self-raising white flour

a pinch of salt

50g (2oz) shredded suet

2 tbsp freshly chopped parsley

2 tbsp freshly chopped thyme

Cock-a-Leekie Soup

1 Put the chicken into a pan in which it fits quite snugly. Add the chopped vegetables, bay leaf and chicken giblets (if available). Add 1.7 litres (3 pints) water and bring to the boil, then reduce the heat, cover the pan and simmer gently for 1 hour.

2 Meanwhile, melt the butter in a large pan, add the leeks and fry gently for 10 minutes or until softened.

3 Remove the chicken from the pan. Strain the stock and set aside. Strip the chicken from the bones and shred roughly. Add to the stock with the prunes and softened leeks.

4 To make the dumplings, sift the flour and salt into a bowl. Stir in the suet, herbs and about 5 tbsp water to make a fairly firm dough. Lightly shape the dough into 2.5cm (1in) balls. Bring the soup just to the boil and season well. Reduce the heat, add the dumplings and cover the pan with a lid. Simmer for about 15–20 minutes until the dumplings are light and fluffy. Serve scattered with chopped parsley.

Serves 8	EASY		NUTRITIONAL INFORMATION
	Preparation Time 30–40 minutes	**Cooking Time** 1 hour 20 minutes	**Per Serving** 280 calories, 4g fat (of which 1g saturates), 40g carbohydrate, 0.2g salt

Cook's Tip

Pesto: put a 20g pack roughly chopped basil into a food processor. Add 25g (1oz) finely grated Parmesan, 50g (2oz) pinenuts and 4 tbsp extra virgin olive oil and whiz to a rough paste. Alternatively, grind in a pestle and mortar. Season with salt and plenty of ground black pepper.

Chicken and Mushroom Broth

4 skinless chicken breasts

pesto (see Cook's Tip), made omitting the Parmesan

1.1 litres (2 pints) chicken stock

100ml (3½fl oz) medium sherry

150g (5oz) exotic mushrooms, cleaned and sliced

1 red chilli, seeded and halved (see page 33)

75g (3oz) conchigliette pasta

2 tbsp soy sauce

a small handful of chopped pak choi or spinach leaves

a dash of Tabasco to serve (optional)

1 Preheat the oven to 200°C (180°C fan oven) mark 6. Make a few slashes in the chicken breasts, then rub the pesto over the chicken, pushing it into the cuts. Put into a roasting tin and roast for 20 minutes.

2 Meanwhile, put the stock into a pan with the sherry and bring to the boil.

3 Add the mushrooms, chilli and pasta. Cover the pan and simmer for 3 minutes until the pasta is cooked. Stir in the soy sauce.

4 Slice the chicken into the broth with the pak choi or spinach.

5 Ladle into warmed bowls and serve immediately. Add a dash of Tabasco if you like it hot!

EASY		NUTRITIONAL INFORMATION		Serves
Preparation Time 20 minutes	**Cooking Time** 20 minutes	**Per Serving** 255 calories, 4.7g fat (of which 1.4g saturates), 16g carbohydrate, 1.4g salt	Dairy free	**4**

Pasta and Chickpea Soup with Pesto

3 tbsp olive oil

1 onion, chopped

2 garlic cloves, finely chopped

1 small leek, trimmed and sliced

1 tsp freshly chopped rosemary

400g can chickpeas

1.2 litres (2 pints) vegetable stock

4 ripe tomatoes, skinned and chopped

1 courgette, diced

125g (4oz) shelled peas

125g (4oz) French beans, halved

125g (4oz) shelled broad beans

50g (2oz) dried pastina (small soup pasta)

2 tbsp freshly chopped parsley

salt and ground black pepper

pesto (see page 67) and freshly grated pecorino or Parmesan to serve

1 Heat the oil in a large saucepan, add the onion, garlic, leek and rosemary and fry gently for 5–6 minutes or until softened but not coloured. Add the chickpeas with their liquid, the stock and tomatoes. Bring to the boil, then reduce the heat, cover the pan and simmer for 40 minutes.

2 Add the courgette, peas, French beans and broad beans. Return to the boil, then reduce the heat and simmer for 10 minutes. Add the pasta and parsley and simmer for 6–8 minutes until al dente. Season to taste with salt and pepper.

3 Ladle into warmed bowls and serve topped with a spoonful of pesto and a sprinkling of cheese.

Serves 6	EASY		NUTRITIONAL INFORMATION	
	Preparation Time 25 minutes	**Cooking Time** about 1 hour	**Per Serving** 211 calories, 8.2g fat (of which 1.2g saturates), 26g carbohydrate, 0.3g salt	Vegetarian

1 tbsp oil

1 medium onion, finely chopped

1 celery stick, chopped

1 leek, trimmed and chopped

1 carrot, chopped

2 red peppers, seeded and diced

225g (8oz) red lentils

400g can chopped tomatoes

1 litre (1³/₄ pints) hot light vegetable stock

25g pack flat-leafed parsley, chopped

salt and ground black pepper

toast to serve

Pepper and Lentil Soup

1 Heat the oil in a pan. Add the onion, celery, leek and carrot and cook for 10–15 minutes until soft.

2 Add the red peppers and cook for 5 minutes. Stir in the red lentils, add the tomatoes and hot stock and season to taste with salt and pepper.

3 Cover the pan and bring to the boil, then reduce the heat and cook, uncovered, for 25 minutes until the lentils are soft and the vegetables are tender.

4 Stir in the parsley. Ladle into warmed bowls and serve with toast.

EASY		NUTRITIONAL INFORMATION		Serves
Preparation Time 15 minutes	**Cooking Time** 45 minutes	**Per Serving** 165 calories, 2.7g fat (of which 0.5g saturates), 26.5g carbohydrate, 0.5g salt	Vegetarian Gluten free • Dairy Free	**6**

Hot and Spicy

Cauliflower Soup

2 x 400ml cans coconut milk

750ml (1¼ pints) vegetable stock

4 garlic cloves, finely chopped

5cm (2in) piece fresh root ginger, peeled and finely chopped

4 lemongrass stalks, roughly chopped

4 kaffir lime leaves, shredded (optional) or zest of 1 lime

4 red chillies

2 tbsp groundnut oil

2 tsp sesame oil

1 large onion, thinly sliced

2 tsp ground turmeric

2 tsp sugar

900g (2lb) cauliflower florets

2 tbsp lime juice

2 tbsp light soy sauce

4 spring onions, shredded

4 tbsp freshly chopped coriander

salt and ground black pepper

1 Put the coconut milk and stock into a pan. Add the garlic and ginger with the lemongrass, lime leaves, if using, or lime zest and chillies. Bring to the boil, then reduce the heat, cover the pan and simmer for 15 minutes. Strain and keep the liquid to one side.

2 Heat the oils together in a clean pan. Add the onion, turmeric and sugar and fry gently for 5 minutes. Add the cauliflower to the pan and stir-fry for 5 minutes or until lightly golden.

3 Add the reserved liquid, the lime juice and soy sauce. Bring to the boil, then reduce the heat, cover the pan and simmer for 10–15 minutes until the cauliflower is tender.

4 Season to taste with salt and pepper, then add the spring onions and coriander to the soup. Ladle into warmed bowls and serve.

Serves	EASY		NUTRITIONAL INFORMATION	
6	**Preparation Time** 25 minutes	**Cooking Time** 40 minutes	**Per Serving** 113 calories, 5g fat (of which 1g saturates), 15g carbohydrate, 1.4g salt	Dairy Free

Thai Chicken Broth

1 tbsp olive oil

4 boneless skinless chicken thighs, around 300g (11oz), shredded

3 garlic cloves, roughly chopped

2 red chillies, seeded and finely diced (see page 33)

1 lemongrass stalk, finely sliced

5cm (2in) piece fresh root ginger, peeled and finely chopped

150ml (¼ pint) white wine

1 litre (1¾ pints) chicken stock

8 fresh coriander sprigs

50g (2oz) rice noodles

125g (4oz) green beans, trimmed and halved

125g (4oz) bean sprouts

4 spring onions, finely sliced

2 tbsp Thai fish sauce (nam pla)

juice of ½ lime

salt and ground black pepper

1 Heat the oil in a large pan over a medium heat. Add the chicken, garlic, chillies, lemongrass and ginger and cook for 3–5 minutes until the chicken is opaque.

2 Add the wine and bring to the boil, then reduce the heat and simmer until reduced by half. Add the stock and bring to the boil. Simmer for 5 minutes or until the chicken is cooked through.

3 Pick the leaves off the coriander and put them to one side. Finely chop the coriander stalks. Add the noodles to the pan and cook for 1 minute, then add the beans and coriander stalks. Cook for 3 minutes.

4 Add the bean sprouts and spring onions (reserving a few to garnish) along with the fish sauce and lime juice. Simmer until heated through, then taste for seasoning. Ladle the noodles and broth into warmed bowls, making sure that each serving has some chicken and bean sprouts. Garnish with the coriander leaves, spring onions and bean sprouts and serve.

EASY		NUTRITIONAL INFORMATION		Serves
Preparation Time 20 minutes	**Cooking Time** 20-25 minutes	**Per Serving** 198 calories, 5g fat (of which 1g saturates), 13g carbohydrate, 1.1g salt	Gluten free • Dairy free	**4**

Pork and Noodle Soup

225g (8oz) minced pork

50g (2oz) peanuts or cashew nuts, roughly chopped

4 garlic cloves, crushed

2 tbsp freshly chopped coriander

1.7 litres (3 pints) chicken stock

3 lemongrass stalks, finely chopped

6 kaffir lime leaves, or zest of 1 large lime

1 tbsp light soy sauce

1 tbsp Thai fish sauce

juice of 2 limes

1 tsp red curry paste or tandoori paste

2 tsp caster sugar

4 tbsp sunflower oil

125g (4oz) rice noodles or egg noodles

125g (4oz) mushrooms, sliced

125g (4oz) broccoli florets

salt and ground black pepper

lime wedges to serve

1 Put the pork into a bowl with the nuts, garlic and coriander and season to taste with salt and pepper. Mix thoroughly, then shape into 18 walnut-sized balls; knead thoroughly with your hands to help bind the mixture and prevent the meatballs breaking up during cooking.

2 Put the stock into a large saucepan with the lemongrass, lime leaves or grated rind, soy sauce, fish sauce, lime juice, curry paste and sugar. Bring to the boil, then reduce the heat, cover the pan and simmer for 20 minutes.

3 Meanwhile, heat 3 tbsp oil in a heavy-based frying pan and fry the meatballs in batches for 4–5 minutes or until golden and cooked through. Set aside.

4 Cook the noodles according to the packet instructions.

5 Meanwhile, heat the remaining oil in the frying pan and stir-fry the mushrooms and broccoli for 1–2 minutes. Drain the noodles and add to the pan with the meatballs. Strain the broth and combine with the pork and noodle mixture.

6 To serve, ladle into warmed bowls and garnish with the lime wedges.

EASY		NUTRITIONAL INFORMATION		Serves
Preparation Time 25 minutes	**Cooking Time** 35 minutes	**Per Serving** 281 calories, 17g fat (of which 3.5g saturates), 19g carbohydrate, 0.8g salt	Dairy free	**6**

15g (½oz) dried porcini or shiitake mushrooms

2 tbsp groundnut oil

225g (8oz) fillet steak, cut into thin strips

1.1 litres (2 pints) beef stock

2 tbsp Thai fish sauce (nam pla), plus extra if needed

1 large fresh red chilli, seeded and finely chopped (see page 33)

1 lemongrass stalk, trimmed and thinly sliced

2.5cm (1in) piece fresh root ginger, peeled and finely chopped

6 spring onions, halved lengthways and cut into 2.5cm (1in) lengths

1 garlic clove, crushed

¼ tsp caster sugar

50g (2oz) medium egg noodles

125g (4oz) fresh spinach leaves, roughly chopped

4 tbsp freshly chopped coriander

ground black pepper

Spicy Beef and Noodle Soup

1 Break the mushrooms into pieces and soak in 150ml (¼ pint) boiling water for 15 minutes.

2 Meanwhile, heat the oil in a large pan over a medium heat, brown the meat in two batches and put aside. Pour the stock into the pan with 2 tbsp fish sauce. Add the mushrooms and their soaking liquid, the chilli, lemongrass, ginger, spring onions, garlic and sugar and bring to the boil.

3 Break the noodles up slightly and add to the pan, then stir gently until they begin to separate. Simmer for 4–5 minutes until the noodles are just tender, stirring occasionally.

4 Stir in the spinach, coriander and reserved steak. Check and adjust the seasoning with pepper and add a little more fish sauce if necessary. Ladle into warmed bowls and serve hot.

Serves 4	EASY		NUTRITIONAL INFORMATION	
	Preparation Time 10 minutes, plus soaking	**Cooking Time** 10 minutes	**Per Serving** 215 calories, 13g fat (of which 3g saturates), 11g carbohydrate, 1.2g salt	Dairy free

Cook's Tip

Courgettes are baby marrows. Look for small, firm vegetables. They lose their flavour as they grow larger.

Spicy Bean and Courgette Soup

2 tbsp olive oil

175g (6oz) onions, finely chopped

2 garlic cloves, crushed

2 tsp ground coriander

1 tbsp paprika

1 tsp mild curry powder

450g (1lb) courgettes, trimmed, halved and sliced

225g (8oz) potatoes, peeled and diced

400g can red kidney beans, drained and rinsed

425g can flageolet beans, drained and rinsed

1.5 litres (2½ pints) vegetable stock

salt and ground black pepper

crusty bread to serve

1 Heat the oil in a pan. Add the onions and garlic and sauté for 2 minutes. Add the spices and cook, stirring, for 1 minute. Mix in the courgettes and potatoes and cook for 1–2 minutes.

2 Add the remaining ingredients and bring to the boil, then reduce the heat, cover the pan and simmer for 25 minutes, stirring occasionally, or until the potatoes are tender. Adjust the seasoning if necessary.

3 Ladle into warmed bowls and serve with crusty bread.

EASY		NUTRITIONAL INFORMATION		Serves
Preparation Time 10 minutes	**Cooking Time** 30 minutes	**Per Serving** 289 calories, 8g fat (of which 1g saturates), 43g carbohydrate, 1.5g salt	Vegetarian Dairy free	**4**

Roasted Onion and Coconut Soup

4 large onions, about 1.1kg (2½lb), halved

2 tsp olive oil

3 large red chillies

6 garlic cloves, unpeeled

½ tsp cumin seeds

900ml (1½ pints) vegetable or chicken stock

2 lemongrass stalks

3 kaffir lime leaves or zest of 1 small lime

2 x 400ml cans coconut milk

salt and ground black pepper

For the Jamaican salsa

1 small banana (optional)

250g (8oz) plum tomatoes, quartered, seeded and finely chopped

1 green chilli, seeded and finely chopped (see page 33)

finely grated zest and juice of 1 lime

2 tbsp freshly chopped coriander

coriander, finely sliced red chilli and coconut milk to serve

1 Preheat the oven to 200°C (180°C fan oven) mark 6. Place the onions in a roasting tin and drizzle with oil. Cook for 20–30 minutes or until brown. Add the chillies, garlic and cumin seeds, cover with foil and cook for 40 minutes or until the onions are soft. Leave to cool.

2 Peel, halve and seed the chillies; discard the seeds. Squeeze the pulp from the garlic and discard the skins. Whiz the chillies, garlic and onions in a food processor until smooth. Transfer the purée to a pan, add the stock, lemongrass and lime leaves or lime zest and season to taste with salt and pepper. Bring slowly to the boil, then reduce the heat, cover the pan and cook gently for 30 minutes.

3 For the salsa, peel the banana, if using, and chop into small pieces. Mix with the tomatoes, chilli, lime zest and juice and coriander.

4 Remove the lemongrass and lime leaves from the soup and discard. Stir in the coconut milk and heat gently. Ladle the soup into warmed bowls and add a spoonful of salsa, garnished with coriander, sliced chilli and a drizzle of coconut milk to each.

Serves	EASY		NUTRITIONAL INFORMATION	
6	**Preparation Time** 25 minutes	**Cooking Time** 1 hour 40 minutes	**Per Serving** 107 calories, 1.9g fat (of which 0.5g saturates), 21g carbohydrate, 0.5g salt	Vegetarian Dairy free

Curried Parsnip Soup

40g (1½ oz) butter

1 onion, sliced

700g (1½lb) parsnips, peeled, cored and finely diced

1 tsp curry powder

½ tsp ground cumin

1.2 litres (2 pints) chicken or vegetable stock

150ml (¼ pint) single cream

salt and ground black pepper

paprika to sprinkle

1 Melt the butter in a large pan, add the onion and fry gently for 5–7 minutes. Add the parsnips and fry gently for about 3 minutes.

2 Stir in the curry powder and cumin and cook for a further 2 minutes.

3 Add the stock, season to taste with salt and pepper and bring to the boil. Reduce the heat, cover the pan and simmer for 35 minutes or until the vegetables are tender.

4 Leave the soup to cool a little, then whiz in batches in a blender or food processor until smooth. Return the soup to the pan and adjust the seasoning. Add the cream and reheat but do not boil.

5 Ladle the soup into warmed bowls, sprinkle with paprika and serve.

Serves 6	EASY		NUTRITIONAL INFORMATION	
	Preparation Time 20 minutes	**Cooking Time** 50 minutes	**Per Serving** 184 calories, 12g fat (of which 7g saturates), 17g carbohydrate, 0.2g salt	Vegetarian

Cook's Tip

Lime Butter: beat the grated zest and juice of ¹/₂ lime into 50g (2oz) softened butter and season to taste with salt and pepper. Shape into a log, wrap in clingfilm and chill until needed. To serve, unwrap and slice thinly.

4 tbsp olive oil

1 onion, chopped

2 garlic cloves, chopped

pinch of crushed red chillies

1 tsp ground coriander

1 tsp ground cumin

¹/₂ tsp ground cinnamon

900ml (1¹/₂ pints) vegetable stock

300ml (¹/₂ pint) tomato juice

1–2 tsp chilli sauce

2 x 400g cans red kidney beans

2 tbsp freshly chopped coriander

salt and ground black pepper

lime butter to serve (optional, see Cook's Tip)

coriander leaves, roughly torn, to garnish

Mexican Bean Soup

1 Heat the oil in a large pan, add the onion, garlic, chilli and spices and fry gently for 5 minutes until lightly golden.

2 Add the stock, tomato juice, chilli sauce and beans with their liquid. Bring to the boil, then reduce the heat, cover the pan and simmer gently for 20 minutes.

3 Leave the soup to cool a little, then whiz in batches in a blender or food processor until very smooth. Return the soup to the pan. Stir in the chopped coriander and heat through, then season to taste with salt and pepper.

4 Ladle the soup into warmed bowls. Top each portion with a few slices of lime butter, if you like, and scatter with torn coriander leaves.

EASY		NUTRITIONAL INFORMATION		Serves
Preparation Time 15 minutes	**Cooking Time** 25 minutes	**Per Serving without lime butter** 184 calories, 8g fat (of which 1.2g saturates), 21g carbohydrate, 1.3g salt	Vegetarian Dairy free	**6**

Mulligatawny Soup

3 rashers streaky bacon, rinded and finely chopped

550g (1¼lb) chicken portions

600ml (1 pint) chicken stock

1 carrot, sliced

1 celery stick, chopped

1 apple, cored and chopped

2 tsp curry powder

4 peppercorns, crushed

1 clove

1 bay leaf

1 tbsp plain flour

150ml (¼ pint) milk

50g (2oz) long-grain rice, cooked, and crusty bread to serve

1 Fry the bacon in a large pan until the fat begins to run. Do not allow the bacon to become brown.

2 Add the chicken and brown well. Drain the meat on kitchen paper and pour off the fat.

3 Return the bacon and chicken to the pan and add the stock and next seven ingredients. Cover the pan and simmer for about 30 minutes or until the chicken is tender.

4 Remove the chicken and allow to cool a little. Cut off the meat and return it to the soup. Discard the clove and bay leaf and reheat the soup gently.

5 Mix the flour with a little cold water. Add to the soup with the milk and reheat without boiling.

6 Ladle the soup into warmed bowls, spoon a mound of rice into each one and serve immediately with crusty bread.

Serves 4	EASY		NUTRITIONAL INFORMATION
	Preparation Time 5 minutes	**Cooking Time** 40 minutes	**Per Serving** 252 calories, 13g fat (of which 4g saturates), 7.3g carbohydrate, 0.9g salt

Goulash Soup

700g (1½lb) silverside or lean chuck steak
25g (1oz) butter
225g (8oz) onions, chopped
1 small green pepper, seeded and chopped
4 tomatoes, skinned and quartered
150g (5oz) tomato purée
600ml (1 pint) rich beef stock
1 tbsp paprika
450g (1lb) potatoes, peeled
150ml (¼ pint) soured cream
salt and ground black pepper
freshly chopped parsley to garnish (optional)

1 Wipe the meat with a damp cloth. Remove any excess fat or gristle and cut the meat into small pieces. Season well with 2 tsp salt and pepper to taste.

2 Melt the butter in a large saucepan, add the onions and green pepper and sauté until tender.

3 Add the meat pieces, tomatoes, tomato purée, stock and paprika. Stir well and bring to the boil, then reduce the heat, cover the pan and simmer for 2½ hours, stirring occasionally.

4 Half an hour before the end of cooking, cut the potatoes into bite-size pieces, bring to the boil in lightly salted water and simmer until cooked. Drain well and add to the soup.

5 Check the seasoning and stir in 2 tbsp soured cream. Ladle into warmed bowls, garnish with chopped parsley, if you like, and serve the remaining soured cream separately, for each person to spoon into their soup.

EASY		NUTRITIONAL INFORMATION		Serves
Preparation Time 20 minutes	**Cooking Time** 2¼ hours	**Per Serving** 594 calories, 30g fat (of which 15g saturates), 35.5g carbohydrate, 1.9g salt	Gluten free	**6**

Hot and Sour Soup

1 tbsp vegetable oil

2 turkey breasts, about 300g (11oz),
or the same quantity of tofu, cut into strips

5cm (2in) piece fresh root ginger, peeled and grated

4 spring onions, finely sliced

1–2 tbsp Thai red curry paste

75g (3oz) long-grain wild rice

1.1 litres (2 pints) hot weak chicken or vegetable stock or
boiling water

200g (7oz) mangetouts, sliced

juice of 1 lime

4 tbsp roughly chopped fresh coriander to garnish

1 Heat the oil in a deep pan. Add the turkey or tofu and cook over a medium heat for 5 minutes or until browned. Add the ginger and spring onions and cook for a further 2–3 minutes. Stir in the curry paste and cook for 1–2 minutes to warm the spices.

2 Add the rice and stir to coat in the curry paste. Pour the hot stock or boiling water into the pan. Stir once and bring to the boil, then reduce the heat, cover the pan and simmer for 20 minutes.

3 Add the mangetouts and cook for a further 5 minutes or until the rice is cooked. Just before serving, squeeze in the lime juice and stir to mix.

4 To serve, ladle into warmed bowls and sprinkle with the coriander.

Serves 4	EASY		NUTRITIONAL INFORMATION	
	Preparation Time 20 minutes	**Cooking Time** 30–35 minutes	**Per Serving** 255 calories, 10g fat (of which 1g saturates), 19g carbohydrate, 0.7g salt	Gluten free • Dairy free

Spiced Dal Soup

125g (4oz) chana dal

1 tsp cumin seeds

2 tsp coriander seeds

1 tsp fenugreek seeds

3 dried red chillies

1 tbsp shredded coconut

2 tbsp ghee or polyunsaturated oil

225g (8oz) tomatoes, skinned and roughly chopped

½ tsp turmeric

1 tsp treacle

coriander sprigs to garnish

lemon wedges to serve

1 Pick over the dal and remove any grit or discoloured pulses. Put into a sieve and wash in cold running water, then drain well and put into a saucepan. Cover with 600ml (1 pint) water and bring to the boil, then reduce the heat, cover the pan and simmer for 1 hour or until tender.

2 Put the cumin, coriander, fenugreek, chillies and coconut into a small electric mill or blender and grind finely. Heat the oil in a heavy-based frying pan, add the spice mixture and fry, stirring, for 30 seconds. Whiz the dal to a purée in a blender or food processor and put into a pan. Stir in the remaining ingredients and 300ml (½ pint) water.

3 Bring to the boil, then reduce the heat, cover the pan and simmer for about 20 minutes. Taste and adjust the seasoning. To serve, ladle into warmed bowls and garnish with coriander sprigs, with lemon wedges to squeeze in.

Serves 4	EASY		NUTRITIONAL INFORMATION	
	Preparation Time 5 minutes	**Cooking Time** 1½ hours	**Per Serving** 172 calories, 8.1g fat (of which 5g saturates), 19g carbohydrate, 0.2g salt	Vegetarian Gluten free

225g (8oz) whole green lentils

4 tbsp sunflower oil

350g (12oz) floury potatoes, peeled and diced

1 large onion, chopped

2 garlic cloves, crushed

¼ tsp ground turmeric

2 tsp ground cumin

50g (2oz) creamed coconut

750ml (1¼ pints) vegetable stock

300ml (½ pint) coconut milk

finely grated zest of 1 lemon

salt and ground black pepper

toasted fresh coconut and coriander sprigs (optional) to garnish

Green Lentil and Coconut Soup

1 Put the lentils into a sieve and wash thoroughly under cold running water. Drain well.

2 Heat the oil in a large saucepan. Add the potatoes and fry gently for 5 minutes until beginning to colour. Remove with a slotted spoon and drain on kitchen paper.

3 Add the onion to the pan and fry gently for 10 minutes until soft. Add the garlic, turmeric and cumin and fry for 2–3 minutes. Add the coconut, stock, coconut milk and lentils and bring to the boil, then reduce the heat, cover the pan and simmer gently for 20 minutes until the lentils are just tender.

4 Add the potatoes and lemon zest and season to taste with salt and pepper. Cook gently for a further 5 minutes until the potatoes are tender. Ladle into warmed bowls, garnish with toasted coconut and the coriander sprigs, if you like, and serve hot.

EASY		NUTRITIONAL INFORMATION		Serves
Preparation Time 20 minutes	**Cooking Time** 40 minutes	**Per Serving** 442 calories, 21.5g fat (of which 9.5g saturates), 48.4g carbohydrate, 0.3g salt	Vegetarian Gluten • Dairy Free	**4**

Curried Mussel Soup

2kg (4½lb) fresh mussels in shells, cleaned
90ml (3fl oz) dry white wine
a pinch of saffron strands
450ml (¾ pint) hot fish or vegetable stock
25g (1oz) butter
4 shallots, finely chopped
1 garlic clove, crushed
1 tsp grated fresh root ginger
½ tsp ground turmeric
½ tsp garam masala
150ml (¼ pint) double cream
1 tbsp freshly chopped parsley or chervil
1 tsp lemon juice, or to taste
ground black pepper
warm crusty bread to serve (optional)

1 Put the mussels into a large pan with the wine. Cover with a tight-fitting lid and steam for 4–5 minutes until the shells have opened, shaking the pan frequently; discard any mussels that remain closed.

2 Meanwhile, put the saffron strands into a bowl, pour on the hot stock and leave to infuse for about 10 minutes.

3 Strain the mussel liquor through a muslin-lined sieve and set aside. Shell the mussels, keeping eight in their shells for the garnish.

4 Melt the butter in a pan, add the shallots, garlic, ginger, turmeric and garam masala and fry gently for 5 minutes until the shallots are soft but not golden. Add the saffron stock and mussel liquor and simmer gently, uncovered, for 10 minutes.

5 Stir in the cream, shelled mussels and parsley or chervil and heat through. Add the lemon juice and season to taste with black pepper.

6 Ladle the soup into warmed bowls and top with the reserved mussels in shells. Serve with warm crusty bread, if you like.

EASY		NUTRITIONAL INFORMATION	Serves
Preparation Time 15 minutes	**Cooking Time** 20 minutes	**Per Serving** 376 calories, 29g fat (of which 15g saturates), 4g carbohydrate, 1g salt	**4**

4

Chilled Soups

Iced Sweet Pepper Soup

4 tbsp freshly chopped coriander

2 medium red peppers, seeded and sliced

1 medium onion, sliced

225g (8oz) ripe tomatoes, sliced

900ml (1½ pints) vegetable stock

150ml (¼ pint) milk

salt and ground black pepper

1 First make coriander ice cubes. Put the chopped coriander into an ice-cube tray, top up with water and freeze.

2 Put the peppers into a large saucepan with the onion, tomatoes and stock. Bring to the boil, then lower the heat, cover the pan and simmer for about 15 minutes or until the vegetables are tender. Drain, reserving the liquid.

3 Whiz the vegetables in a blender or food processor until smooth, then sieve the purée to remove the tomato seeds.

4 Combine the reserved liquid, vegetable purée and milk in a bowl with salt and pepper to taste. Cool for 30 minutes, then chill for at least 2 hours before serving. Ladle into chilled bowls and serve with coriander ice cubes.

Serves 4	EASY		NUTRITIONAL INFORMATION	
	Preparation Time 5 minutes, plus chilling	**Cooking Time** 20 minutes	**Per Serving** 65 calories, 1.5g fat (of which 0.5g saturates), 11g carbohydrate, 0.1g salt	Vegetarian

Chilled Avocado and Lime Soup

1 tbsp extra virgin olive oil

1 bunch of spring onions, trimmed and sliced

225g (8oz) potatoes, peeled and cubed

900ml (1½ pints) vegetable stock

1-2 limes

2 ripe avocados

salt and ground black pepper

snipped chives to garnish

6 bsp very low-fat fromage frais and Melba Toast (see page 40) to serve

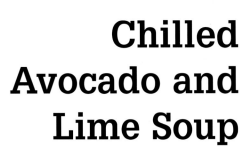

1 Heat the oil in a large saucepan, add the spring onions and fry gently until softened.

2 Add the potatoes to the pan and fry, stirring, for 2 minutes. Add the stock and bring to the boil, then reduce the heat, cover the pan and simmer for 15–20 minutes.

3 Towards the end of the cooking time, remove a little zest from one of the limes, using a zester, and set aside for the garnish. Squeeze the juice from the lime. Halve, stone and peel the avocados, then chop roughly. Add the avocado to the soup with the lime juice. Taste and adjust the seasoning; add extra lime juice (from the other lime) if required.

4 Remove the soup from the heat, allow to cool a little, then whiz in a blender or food processor until smooth. Add 2 tbsp fromage frais and stir to mix. Ladle into soup bowls and chill for 3–4 hours. (The soup thickens as it is chilled.)

5 To serve, add a swirl of fromage frais and a squeeze of lime juice to each bowl. Grind some black pepper on top and garnish with snipped chives and the lime zest. Serve with Melba Toast.

EASY		NUTRITIONAL INFORMATION		Serves
Preparation Time 5–10 minutes, plus chilling	**Cooking Time** 15–20 minutes	**Per Serving** 178 calories, 13g fat (of which 2.6g saturates), 12g carbohydrate, 0.1g salt	Vegetarian	**4**

Chilled Pea Soup with Mint Salsa

450g (1lb) fresh peas in their pods
2 tbsp olive oil
2 leeks, trimmed and sliced
1 garlic clove, crushed
175g (6oz) potato, peeled and cubed
1 litre (1¾ pints) vegetable stock
150ml (¼ pint) double cream
salt and ground black pepper
mint sprigs to garnish

For the mint salsa
juice of 1 lemon
25g (1oz) golden caster sugar
1 small onion, finely chopped
125g (4oz) cucumber, peeled, seeded and diced
4 tbsp freshly chopped mint

1 Remove the peas from their pods, reserving both peas and pods. String the pods and cut into pieces.

2 Heat the oil in a pan, add the leeks, garlic and pea pods and fry gently for 5 minutes. Add the potato and stock and bring to the boil, then reduce the heat, cover the pan and simmer gently for 20 minutes.

3 Leave the soup to cool a little, then whiz in batches in a blender or food processor until smooth. Pass through a fine sieve into the cleaned pan and stir in the fresh peas. Cover and cook gently for a further 10 minutes until the peas are tender.

4 Meanwhile, make the salsa. Put the lemon juice and sugar into a small pan and heat gently to dissolve. Add the onion, cucumber and a pinch of salt. Remove from the heat, stir in the chopped mint and set aside to cool.

5 Season the soup with salt and pepper, cool, then chill for several hours.

6 To serve, stir the cream into the soup and adjust the seasoning. Ladle into bowls and top with the salsa and mint sprigs, adding a few ice cubes, if you like.

Cook's Tip

The pea pods add a depth of flavour and richness to the soup.

EASY		NUTRITIONAL INFORMATION		Serves
Preparation Time 20 minutes, plus chilling	**Cooking Time** 35–40 minutes	**Per Serving** 333 calories, 27g fat (of which 12g saturates), 23g carbohydrate, 0.1g salt	Vegetarian	**4**

Health Tip

Raw garlic is a wonderful tonic for your health and is world-renowned for its curative and protective powers, including lowering blood pressure and cholesterol levels.
Fresh garlic has plump, juicy, mild cloves and is available from May throughout the summer. It is the classic form of garlic to use for making pesto, salsa verde, garlic mayonnaise and chilled soups.

Cucumber, Yogurt and Mint Soup

1 cucumber, coarsely grated

500g (1lb 2oz) Greek yogurt

a generous handful of mint leaves, chopped

1 large garlic clove, crushed

125ml (4fl oz) cold water or light vegetable or chicken stock

salt and ground black pepper

6 ice cubes and mint sprigs to serve

1 Set aside 6 tbsp of the cucumber. Put the remainder into a large bowl with all the remaining ingredients for the soup and mix together. Chill until required.

2 Before serving, stir the soup, then taste and adjust the seasoning. Spoon the soup into six bowls and drop an ice cube, 1 tbsp of the reserved cucumber and a few mint sprigs into each bowl.

Serves	EASY	NUTRITIONAL INFORMATION	
6	**Preparation Time** 15 minutes, plus chilling	**Per Serving** 105 calories, 9g fat (of which 4g saturates), 3g carbohydrate, 0.5g salt	Vegetarian Gluten free

Chilled Leek and Potato Soup with Prawns and Spinach Cream

1kg (2¼ lb) trimmed leeks, chopped
50g (2oz) butter
350g (12oz) onions, roughly chopped
1.1 litres (2 pints) vegetable stock
140ml (4½ fl oz) double cream
225g (8oz) potatoes, peeled and sliced
salt and ground black pepper
cooked peeled prawns and fresh basil sprigs to garnish

For the spinach cream
15g (½ oz) butter
125g (4oz) spinach leaves
zest of 1 lemon
140ml (4½fl oz) double cream

1 Rinse the leeks in cold water, drain and set aside. Melt the butter in a large heavy-based pan and add the onions and leeks. Cook, stirring, for 10 minutes. Add the stock, cream and potatoes and bring to the boil, then reduce the heat, cover the pan and simmer for 30–40 minutes until the vegetables are tender.

2 Leave the soup to cool a little, then whiz in batches in a blender or food processor until smooth. Pass through a fine sieve if you like, then season well with salt and pepper. Chill for 6 hours or overnight.

3 Meanwhile, to make the spinach cream, heat the butter in a pan, add the spinach and lemon zest. Cook, stirring, for 5 minutes. Add the cream and bubble for 1–2 minutes. Whiz in a blender or food processor until smooth. Season to taste with salt and pepper, then chill.

4 Ladle the soup into chilled bowls and spoon in the spinach cream. Garnish with prawns and basil, sprinkle with black pepper and serve.

EASY		NUTRITIONAL INFORMATION		Serves
Preparation Time 20 minutes, plus chilling	**Cooking Time** 40 minutes	**Per Serving** 610 calories, 54g fat (of which 33g saturates) 25g carbohydrate, 1g salt	Gluten free	**4**

Iced Tomato and Herb Soup

450g (1lb) ripe tomatoes
1 small onion, sliced
4 tsp tomato purée
400g can chicken consommé
2 tbsp freshly chopped herbs, such as basil, coriander, parsley
25g (1oz) fresh white breadcrumbs
150ml (¼ pint) soured cream
salt and ground black pepper
fresh basil leaves to garnish

1 Roughly chop the tomatoes and whiz in a blender or food processor with the onion, tomato purée, consommé and herbs until smooth.

2 Rub the tomato mixture through a nylon sieve into a saucepan. Heat gently to remove the frothy texture, then add plenty of salt and pepper.

3 Pour the soup into a large serving bowl and stir in the breadcrumbs. Chill in the refrigerator for at least 2 hours.

4 To serve, stir the soured cream until smooth, then swirl into the soup. Float the fresh basil leaves on top and serve.

Serves 4	EASY	NUTRITIONAL INFORMATION	
	Preparation Time 20 minutes, plus chilling	**Per Serving** 127 calories, 8g fat (of which 4.8g saturates), 11.5g carbohydrate, 0.2g salt	Vegetarian

Chilled Asparagus Soup

1.1kg (2½lb) asparagus, trimmed
3 tbsp olive oil
4 large shallots, finely chopped
200g (7oz) leeks, trimmed and finely chopped
salt and ground black pepper
chervil sprigs to serve

1 Cut the tips off the asparagus and set aside. Cut the stalks into 2.5cm (1in) lengths.

2 Heat the oil in a large pan, add the shallots and cook gently for 2–3 minutes. Add the leeks and cook, stirring occasionally, for about 10 minutes or until they are soft.

3 Add the asparagus stalks and 900ml (1½ pints) water and season to taste with salt and pepper. Bring to the boil, reduce the heat and simmer very gently, uncovered, for 10 minutes or until the asparagus is soft.

4 Leave the soup to cool a little, then whiz in a blender or food processor until smooth. Pour into a bowl and set aside to cool.

5 Add the asparagus tips to a pan of lightly salted boiling water and cook for 2–3 minutes until tender. Drain and refresh under cold running water.

6 Add the asparagus tips to the soup, cover and chill for several hours.

7 To serve, stir about 450ml (¾ pint) iced water into the soup to obtain the required consistency. Season generously with salt and pepper. Ladle into chilled bowls, top with chervil and serve.

Serves 6	EASY		NUTRITIONAL INFORMATION	
	Preparation Time 5 minutes, plus chilling	**Cooking Time** 25 minutes	**Per Serving** 115 calories, 6.8g fat (of which 1g saturates), 7g carbohydrate, 0.4g salt	Vegetarian Gluten free • Dairy free

900g (2lb) ripe tomatoes

4 garlic cloves

50g (2oz) fresh white breadcrumbs

6 tbsp extra virgin olive oil

juice of 1½ small limes

1 red chilli, seeded and chopped (see page 33)

2 cucumbers, seeded and chopped

2 bunches of spring onions, chopped

1 red pepper, seeded and chopped

600ml (1 pint) tomato juice

6 tbsp freshly chopped coriander

salt and ground black pepper

175g bag tortilla chips to serve

To garnish

1 large avocado

juice of ½ small lime

140ml (4½ fl oz) soured cream

a few fresh coriander sprigs

Gazpacho with Tortilla Chips

1 Score a cross in the skin at the base of each tomato, then put into a bowl. Pour over enough boiling water to cover them, leave for 30 seconds, then transfer to a bowl of cold water. Peel, discarding the skins, then cut into quarters. Discard the seeds.

2 Put all the gazpacho ingredients into a large bowl and mix well, then whiz together in batches in a blender or food processor until smooth. Transfer to a bowl or jug, season generously with salt and pepper and stir the soup well. Cover and chill for at least 2 hours or overnight.

3 Just before serving, peel and roughly dice the avocado, then toss in lime juice to coat. Ladle the soup into chilled bowls, garnish with soured cream, the avocado, a sprinkling of black pepper and coriander sprigs and serve the tortilla chips separately.

EASY	NUTRITIONAL INFORMATION		Serves
Preparation Time 25–30 minutes, plus chilling	**Per Serving** 181 calories, 13g fat (of which 2g saturates), 14g carbohydrate, 0.6g salt	Gluten free	**8**

Roasted Vegetable Soup with Olive and Basil Cream

1.4kg (3lb) ripe tomatoes, halved

350g (12oz) shallots or onions, halved

275g (10oz) celery, chopped

4 small garlic cloves

275g (10oz) carrots, sliced

4 red peppers, seeded and chopped

4 tbsp olive oil

2 red chillies

750ml (1¼ pints) passata (see Cook's Tips)

1½ tsp sugar

grated zest and juice of 1 lime

salt and ground black pepper

crushed ice and Olive and Basil Cream (see Cook's Tips) to serve

1 Preheat the oven to 200°C (180°C fan oven) mark 6. Divide all the vegetables between two roasting tins. Add the oil and chillies, then stir well. Roast for 1–1½ hours or until the skins are charred, turning halfway through the cooking time.

2 Discard the chillies. Whiz the vegetables with the passata in a blender or food processor until smooth, then push the purée through a sieve.

3 Add the sugar, lime zest and 2 tbsp juice and plenty of seasoning. Cover and chill.

4 Ladle the soup into chilled bowls, sprinkle with crushed ice and top with Olive and Basil Cream.

Cook's Tips

Passata, a mixture of sieved tomatoes rather like tomato paste, is sold in cartons and bottles. Look out for it in supermarkets.

Olive and Basil Cream: roughly chop 50g (2oz) pitted black olives. Stir into 150ml (¼ pint) crème fraîche with 2 tbsp freshly chopped basil and the grated zest and juice of 1 lemon. Season well with salt and ground black pepper. Cover and chill the cream until ready to serve, then spoon on to the soup.

EASY		NUTRITIONAL INFORMATION		Serves
Preparation Time 15 minutes	**Cooking Time** 1–1½ hours	**Per Serving** 153 calories, 6.7g fat (of which 1.1g saturates), 20.7g carbohydrate, 0.2g salt	Vegetarian Gluten free	**8**

Iced Courgette Soup

50g (2oz) butter or margarine
450g (1lb) courgettes, trimmed and chopped
1 medium potato, peeled and diced
750ml (1¼ pints) vegetable stock or water
1 tsp freshly chopped basil or ½ tsp dried basil
125g (4oz) ripe Blue Brie
salt and ground black pepper
sliced courgettes to serve (optional)

1 Melt the butter or margarine in a large heavy-based saucepan. Add the courgettes and potato, cover the pan and fry gently for about 10 minutes until softened, shaking frequently.

2 Add the stock or water with the basil and season to taste with salt and pepper. Bring to the boil, stirring, then reduce the heat and simmer for 20 minutes until the vegetables are tender.

3 Remove the rind from the Brie and chop the cheese into small dice. Put into a blender or food processor, then pour in the soup and whiz until smooth. Turn into a bowl, cover and leave until cold. Chill in the refrigerator overnight.

4 Whisk the soup vigorously to ensure an even consistency, then taste and adjust the seasoning. Ladle into a chilled soup tureen or individual bowls and float the courgette slices on the top, if you like.

Serves 4	EASY	NUTRITIONAL INFORMATION	
	Preparation Time 40 minutes, plus chilling	**Per Serving** 227 calories, 17.5g fat (of which 11g saturates), 10g carbohydrate, 0.7g salt	Vegetarian

350g (12oz) cooked, peeled beetroot, cut into chunks
juice of ½ lemon
600ml (1 pint) unsweetened apple juice, chilled
200g (7oz) Greek yogurt, chilled
cayenne pepper
10cm (4in) piece cucumber
1 tbsp freshly chopped mint, plus mint sprigs to garnish
salt and ground black pepper

Chilled Beetroot and Apple Soup

1 Put the beetroot into a food processor with the lemon juice, half the apple juice and half the yogurt. Whiz for 1–2 minutes until smooth, then press through a sieve into a bowl.

2 Stir in the remaining apple juice, season to taste with cayenne, salt and pepper and chill.

3 When ready to serve, grate the cucumber into the remaining yogurt and stir in the mint. Ladle the soup into bowls and stir some cucumber yogurt into the middle of each. Sprinkle with a little cayenne pepper, if you like, garnish with mint leaves and serve.

EASY	NUTRITIONAL INFORMATION		Serves
Preparation Time 10 minutes, plus chilling	**Per Serving** 146 calories, 5.5g fat (of which 2.6g saturates), 22.5g carbohydrate, 0.2g salt	Vegetarian Gluten free	**4**

Iced Sorrel Soup

125g (4oz) fresh sorrel
25g (1oz) butter or polyunsaturated margarine
1 medium onion, finely chopped
225g (8oz) potatoes, peeled and finely chopped
750ml (1¼ pints) vegetable stock
150ml (¼ pint) soured cream
salt and ground black pepper
extra virgin olive oil and croûtons to garnish

1 Wash the sorrel leaves thoroughly under cold running water, then roughly shred. Then melt the butter or margarine in a saucepan and fry the onion for 5 minutes until soft.

2 Add the sorrel and cook gently for a further 2–3 minutes until soft. Add the potatoes and stock and season to taste with salt and pepper. Bring to the boil, then reduce the heat, cover the pan and simmer for 20 minutes.

3 Leave the soup to cool a little, then whiz in batches in a blender or food processor until smooth. Stir in the soured cream and chill well.

4 To serve, ladle into bowls, drizzle with oil and garnish with croûtons.

Serves 4	EASY		NUTRITIONAL INFORMATION	
	Preparation Time 5 minutes	**Cooking Time** 30 minutes	**Per Serving** 124 calories, 9g fat (of which 5.5g saturates), 10g carbohydrate, 0.2g salt	Gluten free

5

Feel Good Soups

Autumn Barley Soup

25g (1oz) pot barley, washed and drained

1 litre (1¾ pints) vegetable stock

2 large carrots, diced

1 turnip, peeled and diced

2 leeks, trimmed and sliced

2 celery sticks, diced

1 small onion, finely chopped

1 bouquet garni (see page 59)

ground black pepper

2 tbsp freshly chopped parsley

salt and ground black pepper

1 Put the barley and stock into a saucepan and bring to the boil. Reduce the heat and simmer for 45 minutes until tender.

2 Add the vegetables to the pan with the bouquet garni and season to taste with black pepper. Bring to the boil, then reduce the heat and simmer for about 20 minutes or until the vegetables are tender.

3 Discard the bouquet garni. Add the parsley to the soup, season to taste with salt and pepper and stir well, then ladle into warmed bowls and serve immediately.

EASY		NUTRITIONAL INFORMATION		Serves
Preparation Time 10 minutes	**Cooking Time** 1 hour 5 minutes	**Per Serving** 86 calories, trace fat (of which 0.2g saturates), 17g carbohydrate, 0.1g salt	Vegetarian Dairy free	**4**

Chicken and Bean Soup

1 tbsp olive oil

1 onion, finely chopped

4 celery sticks, chopped

1 red chilli, seeded and roughly chopped
(see page 33)

2 skinless chicken breasts, cut into strips

1 litre (1¾ pints) hot chicken or vegetable stock

100g (3½oz) bulgur wheat

2 x 400g cans cannellini beans, drained

400g can chopped tomatoes

25g (1oz) flat-leafed parsley, roughly chopped

wholegrain bread and hummus to serve

1 Heat the oil in a large heavy-based pan. Add the onion, celery and chilli and cook over a low heat for 10 minutes or until softened. Add the chicken and stir-fry for 3–4 minutes until golden.

2 Add the hot stock to the pan and bring to a simmer. Stir in the bulgur wheat and simmer for 15 minutes. Stir in the cannellini beans and tomatoes and return to a simmer. Sprinkle the chopped parsley over and ladle into warmed bowls. Serve with wholegrain bread and hummus.

Serves 4	EASY		NUTRITIONAL INFORMATION	
	Preparation Time 10 minutes	**Cooking Time** 30 minutes	**Per Serving** 351 calories, 6g fat (of which 1g saturates), 48g carbohydrate, 2.7g salt	Dairy free

1 tbsp olive oil

about 300g (11oz) boneless skinless chicken thighs, cubed

3 garlic cloves, crushed

2 medium red chillies, seeded and finely diced (see page 33)

1 litre (1³⁄₄ pints) chicken stock

250g (9oz) each green beans, broccoli, sugarsnap peas and courgettes, chopped

50g (2oz) wheat-free pasta shapes or spaghetti, broken into short lengths

Chicken Broth

1 Heat the oil in a large pan, add the chicken, garlic and chillies and cook for 5–10 minutes or until the chicken is opaque all over.

2 Add the stock and bring to the boil, then add the vegetables, reduce the heat and simmer for 5 minutes or until the chicken is cooked through.

3 Meanwhile, cook the pasta in a separate pan of lightly salted boiling water until just cooked – 5–10 minutes, depending on the type of pasta.

4 Drain the pasta and add to the broth. Ladle into warmed bowls and serve immediately.

EASY		**NUTRITIONAL INFORMATION**		**Serves**
Preparation Time 30 minutes	**Cooking Time** 15 minutes	**Per Serving** 229 calories, 7g fat (of which 1g saturates), 16g carbohydrate, 1.2g salt	Dairy free	**4**

Full-of-goodness Broth

1–2 tbsp medium curry paste
200ml (7fl oz) reduced-fat coconut milk
600ml (1 pint) hot vegetable stock
200g (7oz) smoked tofu, cubed
2 pak choi, chopped
a handful of sugarsnap peas
4 spring onions, chopped
lime wedges to serve

1 Heat the curry paste in a pan for 1–2 minutes. Add the coconut milk and hot stock and bring to the boil.

2 Add the smoked tofu, pak choi, sugarsnap peas and spring onions, reduce the heat and simmer for 1–2 minutes.

3 Ladle into warmed bowls and serve with a wedge of lime to squeeze in.

Try Something Different

Replace the smoked tofu with shredded leftover roast chicken and simmer for 2–3 minutes.

EASY		NUTRITIONAL INFORMATION		Serves
Preparation Time 10 minutes	**Cooking Time** 6-8 minutes	**Per Serving** 107 calories, 4g fat (of which trace saturates), 9g carbohydrate, 1g salt	Vegetarian Gluten free • Dairy free	**4**

Cream of Parsley Soup

50g (2oz) butter or polyunsaturated margarine
225g (8oz) parsley, roughly chopped
2 medium onions, sliced
125g (4oz) celery, sliced
3 tbsp plain wholemeal flour
2 litres (3½ pints) vegetable stock
150ml (¼ pint) single cream
salt and ground black pepper
parsley sprigs to garnish

1 Melt the butter or margarine in a large saucepan and add the parsley, onions and celery. Cover the pan and cook gently for about 10 minutes until the vegetables are soft. Shake the pan occasionally.

2 Stir in the flour until smooth, then mix in the stock. Add salt and pepper to taste and bring to the boil, then reduce the heat, cover the pan and simmer for 25–30 minutes.

3 Leave the soup to cool a little, then whiz in batches in a blender or food processor until smooth. Leave to cool completely, then chill.

4 Reheat until bubbling, then taste and adjust the seasoning and swirl in the cream. Ladle into warmed bowls, garnish with parsley sprigs and serve.

Serves 8	EASY		NUTRITIONAL INFORMATION	
	Preparation Time 15 minutes, plus chilling	**Cooking Time** 45 minutes	**Per Serving** 137 calories, 9.5g fat (of which 5.6g saturates), 10.5g carbohydrate, 0.5g salt	Vegetarian

Cook's Tip

Miso (fermented barley and soya beans) is a living food in the same way that yogurt is and contains bacteria and enzymes that are destroyed by boiling. Miso is best added as a flavouring at the end of cooking. It's available from Asian shops and larger supermarkets.

Mushroom, Spinach and Miso Soup

1 tbsp vegetable oil

1 onion, finely sliced

125g (4oz) shiitake mushrooms, finely sliced

225g (8oz) baby spinach leaves

1.1 litres (2 pints) fresh fish stock

4 tbsp mugi miso (see Cook's Tip)

1 Heat the oil in a large pan over a low heat, add the onion and cook gently for 15 minutes until soft.

2 Add the mushrooms and cook for 5 minutes, then stir in the spinach and stock. Heat for 3 minutes, then stir in the miso – don't boil, as miso is a live culture. Ladle the soup into warmed bowls and serve hot.

Serves 6	EASY		NUTRITIONAL INFORMATION	
	Preparation Time 5 minutes	**Cooking Time** 25 minutes	**Per Serving** 55 calories, 2g fat (of which trace saturates), 6g carbohydrate, 1.3g salt	Gluten free • Dairy free

4 tbsp extra virgin olive oil, plus extra to serve

1 onion, finely chopped

2 garlic cloves, crushed

2 tsp freshly chopped thyme or a large pinch of dried thyme

2 tsp freshly chopped rosemary or a large pinch of dried rosemary

zest of ½ lemon

2 tsp ground coriander

¼ tsp cayenne pepper

125g (4oz) arborio rice

1.1 litres (2 pints) vegetable stock

225g (8oz) fresh or frozen and thawed spinach, shredded

4 tbsp pesto (see page 67)

salt and ground black pepper

freshly grated Parmesan to serve

Spinach and Rice Soup

1 Heat half the oil in a pan. Add the onion, garlic, herbs, lemon zest and spices, then fry gently for 5 minutes.

2 Add the remaining oil with the rice and cook, stirring, for 1 minute. Add the stock and bring to the boil, then reduce the heat and simmer gently for 20 minutes or until the rice is tender.

3 Stir the spinach into the soup with the pesto. Cook for 2 minutes, then season to taste with salt and pepper.

4 Ladle into warmed bowls and serve drizzled with a little oil and topped with Parmesan.

EASY		NUTRITIONAL INFORMATION		Serves
Preparation Time 10 minutes	**Cooking Time** 25–30 minutes	**Per Serving** 335 calories, 20g fat (of which 4g saturates), 29g carbohydrate, 0.7g salt	Vegetarian Gluten free	**4**

Spring Vegetable Broth

1 tbsp olive oil
4 shallots, chopped
1 fennel bulb, chopped
1 leek, trimmed and chopped
5 small carrots, chopped
1.1 litres (2 pints) hot chicken stock
2 courgettes, chopped
1 bunch of asparagus, chopped
2 x 400g cans cannellini beans, drained and rinsed
50g (2oz) Gruyère or Parmesan cheese shavings to serve

1 Heat the oil in a large pan. Add the shallots, fennel, leek and carrots and fry for 5 minutes or until they start to soften.

2 Add the hot stock, cover and bring to the boil. Add the courgettes, asparagus and beans, then reduce the heat and simmer for 5–6 minutes until the vegetables are tender.

3 Ladle into warmed bowls, sprinkle with a little cheese and serve.

Variation

This broth is also good with a tablespoon of pesto (see page 67) added to each bowl and served with chunks of crusty bread.

EASY		NUTRITIONAL INFORMATION		Serves
Preparation Time 20 minutes	**Cooking Time** 20 minutes	**Per Serving** 264 calories, 6g fat (of which 3g saturates), 35g carbohydrate, 2.4g salt	Dairy free	**4**

Try Something Different

Instead of celery, use 500g (1lb 2oz) celeriac, peeled and diced.
Replace the sage with 2 tsp freshly chopped thyme.

Celery Soup

25g (1oz) butter
1 tbsp olive oil
1 medium leek, trimmed and sliced
6 celery sticks, finely sliced
1 tbsp finely chopped sage
600ml (1 pint) hot chicken stock
300ml (½ pint) milk
salt and ground black pepper
basil sprigs to garnish

1 Melt the butter in a pan and add the oil. Add the leek and fry for 10–15 minutes until soft. Add the celery and sage and cook for 5 minutes to soften.

2 Add the hot stock and milk to the pan, then season with salt and pepper, cover and bring to the boil. Reduce the heat and simmer for 10–15 minutes until the celery is tender.

3 Leave the soup to cool a little, then whiz in batches in a blender or food processor until smooth. Return the soup to the pan, reheat gently and season with salt and pepper.

4 Ladle into warmed bowls, sprinkle with black pepper, garnish with basil sprigs and serve.

Serves 4	EASY		NUTRITIONAL INFORMATION	
	Preparation Time 10 minutes	**Cooking Time** 30–40 minutes	**Per Serving** 123 calories, 10g fat (of which 5g saturates), 6g carbohydrate, 0.8g salt	Gluten free

Cook's Tip

Once you have added the eggs, don't boil the soup or the eggs will curdle.

1.7 litres (3 pints) chicken stock

150g (5oz) orzo or other dried soup pasta

3 medium eggs

juice of 1 large lemon

2 tbsp finely chopped fresh chives

2 tbsp finely chopped fresh chervil

salt and ground black pepper

lemon wedges to serve

Herb and Lemon Soup

1 Bring the stock to the boil in a large pan. Add the pasta and cook for 5 minutes or according to the packet instructions.

2 Beat the eggs in a bowl until frothy, then add the lemon juice and 1 tbsp cold water. Slowly stir in two ladlefuls of the hot stock. Put the egg mixture into the pan with the rest of the stock, then warm through over a very low heat for 2–3 minutes.

3 Add the chives and chervil and season with salt and pepper. Ladle the soup into warmed bowls and serve immediately, with lemon wedges.

EASY		NUTRITIONAL INFORMATION		Serves
Preparation Time 10 minutes	**Cooking Time** 15 minutes	**Per Serving** 130 calories, 4g fat (of which 1g saturates), 18g carbohydrate, 1.8g salt	Dairy free	**6**

Summer Vegetable Soup with Herb Pistou

3 tbsp sunflower oil

1 onion, finely chopped

225g (8oz) waxy potatoes, peeled and finely diced

175g (6oz) carrots, finely diced

1 medium turnip, finely diced

4 bay leaves

6 large fresh sage leaves

2 courgettes, about 375g (13oz), finely diced

175g (6oz) green beans, trimmed and halved

125g (4oz) shelled small peas

225g (8oz) tomatoes, seeded and finely diced

1 small broccoli head, broken into florets

salt and ground black pepper

Pistou (see Cook's Tip) or ready-made pesto (see page 67) to serve

1 Heat the oil in a large pan over a gentle heat. Add the onion, potatoes, carrots and turnip and cook for 10 minutes. Pour in 1.7 litres (3 pints) cold water and season with salt and pepper. Bring to the boil and add the bay and sage leaves, then reduce the heat and simmer for 25 minutes.

2 Add the courgettes, beans, peas and tomatoes. Bring back to the boil, then reduce the heat and simmer for 10–15 minutes. Add the broccoli 5 minutes before the end of the cooking time.

3 Remove the bay and sage leaves and adjust the seasoning. Ladle the soup into warmed bowls and serve immediately, with the pistou or pesto on the side to stir into the hot soup.

Cook's Tip

Pistou is a Provençal condiment similar to Italian pesto. To make your own, using a pestle and mortar, or a small bowl and the end of a rolling pin, or a mini processor, pound together $3/4$ tsp sea salt and 6 chopped garlic cloves until smooth. Add 15g ($1/2$oz) freshly chopped basil and pound to a paste, then mix in 12 tbsp olive oil, a little at a time. Store in a sealed jar in the refrigerator for up to one week.

Serves	EASY		NUTRITIONAL INFORMATION	
6	Preparation Time 20 minutes	Cooking Time 1 hour	Per Serving 163 calories, 7g fat (of which 1g saturates), 17g carbohydrate, 0.1g salt	Vegetarian Gluten free • Dairy free

50g (2oz) butter

350g (12oz) lettuce leaves, roughly chopped

125g (4oz) spring onions, trimmed and roughly chopped

1 tbsp plain wholemeal flour

600ml (1 pint) vegetable stock

150ml (¼ pint) milk

salt and ground black pepper

soured cream to serve (optional)

Lettuce Soup

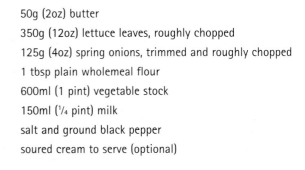

1 Melt the butter in a deep saucepan, add the lettuce and spring onions and cook gently for about 10 minutes until very soft.

2 Stir in the flour and cook, stirring, for 1 minute, then add the stock. Bring to the boil, then reduce the heat, cover the pan and simmer for 45 minutes to 1 hour.

3 Leave the soup to cool a little, when whiz in batches in a blender or food processor until smooth. Return to the rinsed-out pan and add the milk with salt and pepper to taste. Reheat to serving temperature.

4 Ladle into warmed bowls and finish with a swirl of soured cream, if you like.

Serves 4	EASY		NUTRITIONAL INFORMATION	
	Preparation Time 5 minutes	**Cooking Time** 1–1¼ hours	**Per Serving** 139 calories, 11.5g fat (of which 7.5g saturates), 6.5g carbohydrate, 0.3g salt	Vegetarian

Index